P9-DHP-099

Common Marsh,
Underwater and
Floating-leaved
Plants of the
United States and Canada

Common Marsh, Underwater and Floating-leaved Plants of the United States and Canada

NEIL HOTCHKISS

Wildlife Biologist
Patuxent Wildlife Research Center,
Laurel, Maryland

DOVER PUBLICATIONS, INC., NEW YORK

Published in Canada by General Publishing Company, Ltd., 30 Lesmill Road, Don Mills, Toronto, Ontario.

Published in the United Kingdom by Constable and Company, Ltd., 10 Orange Street, London WC 2.

Common Marsh, Underwater and Floating-leaved Plants of the United States and Canada (first Dover edition, 1972) is an unabridged and unaltered republication of the following two publications of the Bureau of Sport Fisheries and Wildlife, United States Department of the Interior:

Common Marsh Plants of the United States and Canada by Neil Hotchkiss, Resource Publication 93, December 1970.

Underwater and Floating-leaved Plants of the United States and Canada by Neil Hotchkiss, Resource Publication 44, May 1967.

International Standard Book Number: 0-486-22810-X
Library of Congress Catalog Card Number: 74-187019

Manufactured in the United States of America
Dover Publications, Inc.
180 Varick Street
New York, N. Y. 10014

Common Marsh
Plants of the
United States and Canada

CONTENTS

COMMON MARSH PLANTS
OF THE UNITED STATES AND CANADA

This is the fourth of a series of publications on field identification of North American marsh and water plants. It describes the
emergent and semiemergent plants most likely to be found in inland
and coastal marshes. It omits hundreds of uncommon marsh plants and
plants less characteristic of marshes than of marsh edges, lake and
stream shores, or wet meadows.

The first of the series, "Pondweeds and Pondweedlike Plants of
Eastern North America," Circular 187, was broadened in scope as
Resource Publication 44, "Underwater and Floating-leaved Plants of
the United States and Canada," and is superseded by it. The present
publication, widens the scope of "Bulrushes and Bulrushlike Plants
of Eastern North America," Circular 221, and contains most of the
species listed therein.

This guide is designed for identification of marsh plants
without recourse to technical botanical keys. To use it, read
pages 1 to 4 and then look at the drawings. To identify a plant,
find the group in which it fits, then find a drawing and description
that match it.

Each description is headed by a common name and a scientific
name. In parentheses are alternative names used by Merritt Lyndon
Fernald in "Gray's Manual of Botany, Eighth Edition" (1950), by
Herbert L. Mason in "A Flora of the Marshes of California" (1957),
and by John Kunkel Small in "Manual of the Southeastern Flora" (1933).

Because of low temperature and infertile soil, marsh plants are
scarce east of the Mackenzie River Valley and north of the latitude
of James Bay. Elsewhere they grow wherever soil is saturated or
shallowly flooded with fresh or brackish water. Inland, most marshes
have less water in summer than at other times. Along the coasts, the
water level in many marshes changes twice a day with the tides; in
other marshes, nearly cut off from the ocean, the water level is
relatively constant. A few kinds of plants tolerate high salinity at
the edge of the ocean and a few tolerate high alkalinity inland, but
most kinds live only in fresh or slightly brackish water.

Marsh plants differ in height, from short plants that carpet the ground to plants three times the height of a man. Even one kind may vary widely in height or shape with different water or soil conditions, if it is crowded, or if it is damaged by man or animals. Most marsh plants grow upright; a few grow horizontally or lean on other plants. Most kinds live underground through winter and send up new aerial stems each spring; but Wildrice, Wild Millet, Walter Millet, some Smartweeds, and a few other plants come up from seed each year.

Seeds of Bulrushes, Threesquares, Spikerushes, Wildrice, Rice, Millets, and Smartweeds are important duck foods; and rootstocks and tubers of several kinds of marsh plants are important foods for wild geese and muskrats. Each plant described is food or shelter for animals while it is alive; is food for bacteria and protozoa and finally fishes after it dies. In shallow water, marsh plants help stabilize mud and sand bottoms and help protect shores from wave erosion.

The plants are discussed in seven groups. Within each group, the kinds which resemble one another most closely are next to each other; wide-ranging kinds usually precede those with a smaller range; and northern kinds usually precede southern.

Group 1. Plants with upright or upslanted leafless stems; or similar plants with long, narrow leaves coming from the lower part of the stems; flowers usually individually inconspicuous, but crowded and numerous (showy in Flowering-rush and Swamp-lily) (pages 5 to 22)

Softstem Bulrush
Hardstem Bulrush
Slender Bulrush
Southern Bulrush
Swamp Bulrush
Saltmarsh Fimbristylis
Baltic Rush
Soft Rush
Soldier Rush
Needlerush
Bog Rush
Blackgrass
Seaside Arrowgrass
Southern Arrowgrass
Flowering-rush
Common Threesquare
Olney Threesquare
Torrey Threesquare
Ricefield Bulrush
Bluntscale Bulrush
Rush Fuirena
Slender Spikerush
Dwarf Spikerush

Trianglestem Spikerush
Water Spikerush
Common Spikerush
Walking Spikerush
Blunt Spikerush
Saltmarsh Spikerush
Squarestem Spikerush
Northern Jointed Spikerush
Southern Jointed Spikerush
Gulf Spikerush
Broadleaf Cattail
Narrowleaf Cattail
Southern Cattail
Blue Cattail
Big Burreed
Eastern Burreed
Shining Burreed
Slender Burreed
Floating Burreed
Little Burreed
Sweetflag
Swamp-lily

Group 2. Plants with upright or upslanted stems with grasslike leaves on two sides (one plane); flowers individually inconspicuous between scales which overlap in two rows to form spikelets; the spikelets clustered toward the top of stems (pages 23 to 36)

Phragmites	Rice Cutgrass
Tufted Hairgrass	Southern Cutgrass
Whitetop	Sloughgrass
Reed Mannagrass	Saltgrass
Western Mannagrass	Coast Dropseed
Low Mannagrass	Giant Setaria
Water Mannagrass	Sacciolepis
Sharpscale Mannagrass	Jointgrass
Bearded Sprangletop	Maidencane
Wildrice	Water Panicum
Giant Cutgrass	Prairie Cordgrass
Rice	Big Cordgrass
Wild Millet	Saltmeadow Cordgrass
Walter Millet	Saltmarsh Cordgrass
Reed Canarygrass	California Cordgrass

Group 3. Plants with upright stems with grasslike leaves on three sides; flowers individually inconspicuous between scales which usually overlap in several rows to form spikelets (two rows in Redroot Cyperus); the spikelets clustered toward the top of stems (pages 37 to 45)

Beaked Sedge	River Bulrush
Slough Sedge	Tuberous Bulrush
Lake Sedge	Saltmarsh Bulrush
Lyngbye Sedge	Redroot Cyperus
Pacific Sedge	Twig-rush
Saltmarsh Sedge	Sawgrass
Alkali Bulrush	Everglade Beakrush

Group 4. Plants with upright, sprawling, or horizontal stems with singly placed, nongrasslike, lance-shaped or wider, untoothed leaves; flowers clustered at the end of stems or single or clustered at the base of leaves (pages 46-55)

Water Smartweed	Roundleaf Mudplantain
Marsh Smartweed	Floating Waterprimrose
Nodding Smartweed	Marsh Dayflower
Swamp Smartweed	Marsh Boltonia
Dotted Smartweed	Atlantic Sea-blite
Southern Smartweed	Tidemarsh Waterhemp
Hairy Smartweed	Annual Saltmarsh Aster
Halberdleaf Tear-thumb	Perennial Saltmarsh Aster
Longleaf Mudplantain	

Group 5. Plants with upright, sprawling, or horizontal stems with paired, whorled, or otherwise clustered, lance-shaped or wider, untoothed leaves (sometimes little teeth in Sea-oxeye); or plants with leafless stems and paired or whorled branches; flowers single or clustered at the end of stems, in stalked heads along stems, or single or clustered at the base of leaves (pages 56-69)

Marestail	Alligatorweed
Water Horsetail	Jaumea
Slender Glasswort	Saltwort
Bigelow Glasswort	Saltflat-grass
Woody Glasswort	Frankenia
California Glasswort	Seaside Gerardia
Marsh-purslane	Saltmarsh Loosestrife
Goldenpert	Little Sea-pink
Purple Loosestrife	Big Sea-pink
Swamp Loosestrife	Coast Milkweed
Waterwillow	Sea-oxeye
Creeping Rush	Coast Bacopa
Lemon Bacopa	

Group 6. Plants with both their lance-shaped or wider, untoothed leaves and the stalks of their solitary flowers or flower clusters coming from underground stems or underwater stems (pages 70 to 86)

Spatterdock	Bulltongue
American Lotus	Broadleaf Waterplantain
Pickerelweed	Narrowleaf Waterplantain
Arrow-arum	Upright Burhead
Northern Arrowhead	Creeping Burhead
Broadleaf Arrowhead	Damasonium
Engelmann Arrowhead	Sea-lavender
Hooded Arrowhead	Goldenclub
Long-barb Arrowhead	American Frogbit
Bur Arrowhead	Water-hyacinth
Slender Arrowhead	Waterlettuce
Delta Duckpotato	

Group 7. Plants with tooth-edged to deeply divided leaves or leaflets (pages 87 to 94)

Marsh Cinquefoil	Water-parsley
Waterparsnip	Marsh Hibiscus
Bulblet Waterhemlock	Saltmarsh Pluchea
Nodding Beggarticks	Mock-bishopweed
Marsh Mermaidweed	Marsh Eryngo
Cutleaf Mermaidweed	Saltmarsh Mallow
Parrotfeather	

Group 1. <u>PLANTS WITH UPRIGHT OR UPSLANTED LEAFLESS STEMS; OR
SIMILAR PLANTS WITH LONG, NARROW LEAVES COMING FROM THE LOWER PART OF
THE STEMS; FLOWERS USUALLY INDIVIDUALLY INCONSPICUOUS, BUT CROWDED AND
NUMEROUS</u>; growing inland in fresh and moderately alkali marshes and
along the coasts in fresh to salt marshes. Stems or leaves usually
stand close to each other in colonies and come up year after year from
rootstocks. They vary from sometimes under water in a few kinds to
more than twice as high as a man in Hardstem Bulrush. Flowering-rush
has showy pink flowers, Swamp-lily showy white ones. The rest have inconspicuous flowers in greenish, yellowish, or brown clusters. Flowers
are often lacking; then identification of Bulrushes, Spikerushes,
Cattails, and Burreeds is difficult.

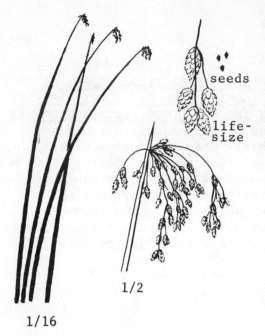

1/16

seeds

life-
size

1/2

SOFTSTEM BULRUSH, Scirpus validus
(Scirpus steinmetzii)

Inland fresh marshes and coastal fresh and brackish marshes; Alaska to Newfoundland and the southernmost States.

Stems waist-high to twice as high as a man, often leaning, usually grayish-green and easily curshed between fingers, round in cross section. Cluster of spikelets usually droopy. Spikelets reddish-brown, their scales about the same length as the brownish-gray ripe seeds which are partly exposed beneath them, a seed under each scale.

Resembles Hardstem, Slender, and Southern Bulrushes; but those species usually have dark-green, firm stems; and Hardstem has stiff-branched clusters of larger, longer-scaled spikelets; Slender has singly placed spikelets; Southern has bluntly triangular stems.

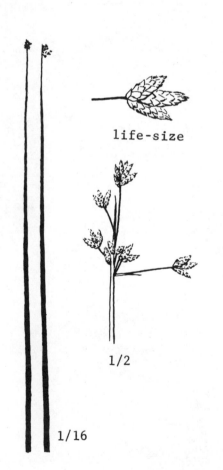

life-size

1/2

1/16

HARDSTEM BULRUSH, Scirpus acutus

Inland fresh and alkali marshes and coastal fresh and brackish marshes; British Columbia to Newfoundland, California, Texas, and North Carolina.

Stems as high as a man to more than twice as high, usually upright, usually dark-green and not easily crushed between fingers, round in cross section. Cluster of spikelets stiff-branched. Spikelets usually dull-brown, their scales much longer than the seeds hidden beneath them. Seeds similar to Softstem Bulrush.

Resembles Softstem, Slender, and Southern Bulrushes; but those species usually have droopy clusters of smaller spikelets; and Softstem usually has grayish-green soft stems and smaller, shorter-scaled spikelets; Slender has singly placed spikelets; Southern has bluntly triangular stems.

6

SLENDER BULRUSH, Scirpus heterochaetus

Inland fresh marshes; Washington to Quebec, Oregon, Tennessee, and New York.

Stems similar to Hardstem Bulrush, except usually slimmer and shorter. Cluster of spikelets usually droopy. Spikelets light-brown, singly placed. Seeds similar to Softstem Bulrush.

Resembles Softstem, Hardstem, and Southern Bulrushes, but those species have some spikelets bunched; Softstem usually has grayish-green soft stems; Hardstem has stiff-branched clusters of spikelets; Southern has bluntly triangular stems.

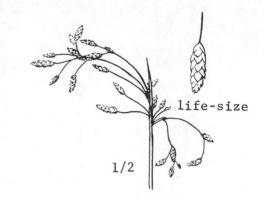

life-size

1/2

SOUTHERN BULRUSH, Scirpus californicus

Inland fresh and alkali marshes and coastal fresh and brackish marshes; California to South Carolina, Texas, and Florida.

Stems similar to Hardstem Bulrush, but bluntly triangular in cross section. Cluster of spikelets usually droopy. Spikelets reddish-brown, stalkless or nearly so. Seeds similar to Softstem Bulrush.

Resembles Softstem, Hardstem, and Slender Bulrushes, but those species have stems which are round in cross section; Softstem usually has grayish-green soft stems; Hardstem has stiff-branched clusters of spikelets; Slender has singly placed spikelets.

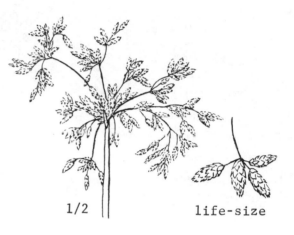

1/2   life-size

SWAMP BULRUSH, Scirpus etuberculatus

Inland and rarely coastal fresh marshes; Missouri; Delaware to Florida and Louisiana.

Stems waist-high to as high as a man, with 1 to 3 long leaves coming from near their base. Spikelets greenish-brown. Ripe seeds dark-brown.

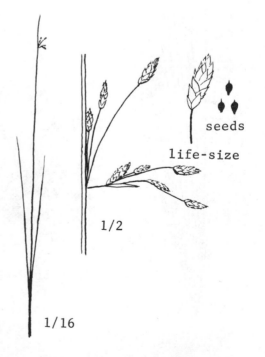

seeds

life-size

1/2

1/16

7

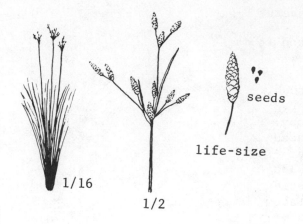

seeds

life-size

1/16

1/2

SALTMARSH FIMBRISTYLIS,
Fimbristylis spadicea
(Fimbristylis castanea)

Coastal salt and brackish
marshes; New York to Florida
and Texas.
Stems less than knee-high
to waist-high, usually in
clumps with many wiry basal
leaves. Spikelets brown,
oval or oblong. Ripe seeds
brown.

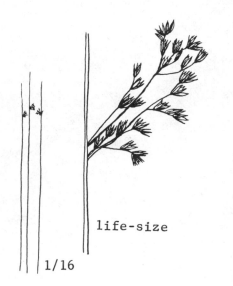

life-size

1/16

BALTIC RUSH, Juncus balticus
(Juncus leseurii, mexicanus,
and textilis)

Inland fresh and alkali
marshes; Alaska to Labrador,
California, Texas, and Pennsylvania.
Stems less than knee-high
to as high as a man, not in
big clumps. Flower clusters
greenish to dark-brown, each
long-lasting flower with 3
taper-tipped sepals and 3
similar petals.

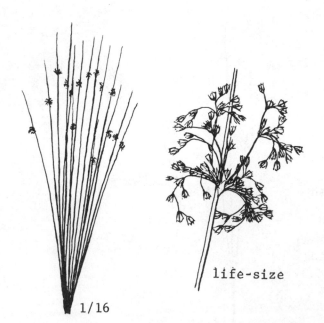

life-size

1/16

SOFT RUSH, Juncus effusus

Inland fresh marshes;
Alaska to Newfoundland and
the southernmost States
(commonest in eastern half
of United States).
Stems knee-high to as high
as a man, in big clumps.
Flower clusters greenish to
brown. Flowers similar to
those of Baltic Rush, except
smaller and usually lighter-
colored.

SOLDIER RUSH
Juncus militaris

Inland fresh marshes;
Ontario to Newfoundland,
Indiana, and Maryland.
Stems less than knee-
high to waist-high,
topped with a brown clus-
ter of flowers, and with
a long midstem leaf
standing high above it.
Often there are limp
threadlike underwater
leaves. Flowers are in
bunches within a cluster.
Individually they re-
semble flowers of
Baltic Rush.

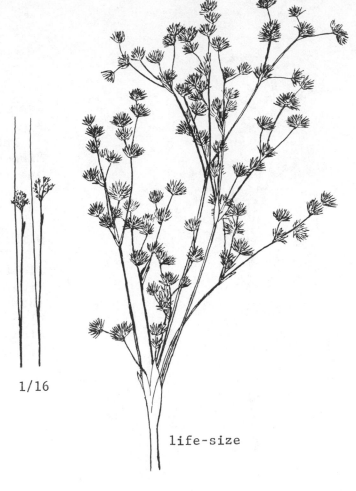

1/16

life-size

NEEDLERUSH,
Juncus roemerianus

Coastal brackish and
salt marshes; Maryland
to Texas.
Stems and stemlike
leaves knee-high to
shoulder-high, usually in
dark-green or dark-gray
colonies which look about
the same the year around.
Tips of stems and leaves
are so hard and sharp that
they often puncture skin.
Flower clusters brown.
Flowers are in bunches
within a cluster. In-
dividually they resemble
flowers of Baltic Rush.

1/16

life-size

BOG RUSH, Juncus pelocarpus

Inland fresh marshes;
Minnesota to Labrador, Indiana, and Maryland.
    Stems ankle-high to less
than knee-high. Flower clusters greenish, each flower
with 3 blunt-tipped sepals
and 3 similar petals.
Plants often have tufts of
tiny leaves where the drawing
shows flowers. Underwater
plants are merely small
clumps of tapered leaves.

life-size   life-size

BLACKGRASS, Juncus gerardi

    Coastal brackish marshes and rarely
inland brackish marshes; British Columbia
to Washington; Utah; North Dakota to Newfoundland, Illinois, and Virginia.
    Stems ankle-high to waist-high, with a
few long leaves coming from near the base.
Flowers have lengthwise dark-brown and yellowish stripes,   each flower with 3 blunt-
tipped sepals and 3 similar petals.

life-
size

SEASIDE ARROWGRASS, Triglochin maritima
        (Triglochin concinna)

   Inland fresh, brackish, and alkali
marshes and coastal brackish and salt
marshes; Alaska to Newfoundland, California, New Mexico, Nebraska, and Delaware.
   Stems ankle-high to waist-high.
Leaves about as thick as the stems.
Tiny greenish flowers produce a seed pods
which are oval in side view and 6-sided
or triangular in end view. Ripe pods
split lengthwise into 6 parts, each containing one seed.

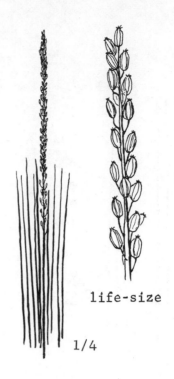

life-size

1/4

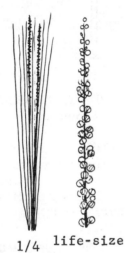

1/4 life-size

SOUTHERN ARROWGRASS, Triglochin striata

   Coastal brackish and salt marshes; Oregon to California; Delaware to Louisiana.
   Resembles Seaside Arrowgrass, but
Southern Arrowgrass is less than knee-high,
and its ripe seed pods are roundish in side
view and triangular in end view and they
split lengthwise into 3 parts.

FLOWERING-RUSH, Butomus umbellatus

   This native of Europe is common
in fresh marshes along the tidal
St. Lawrence River and has been
found west to Illinois and in
Idaho.
   Stems knee-high to shoulder-
high, topped with a cluster of
pink flowers. Leaves about the
same thickness as stems. Six pods
develop in the center of each
flower.   Nonflowering plants with
limp leaves are occasional under
water.

1/4

life-size

1/16

11

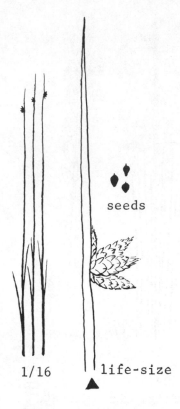

seeds

1/16 | life-size ▲

COMMON THREESQUARE,
Scirpus americanus

Inland fresh and alkali
marshes and coastal fresh,
brackish, and (on Pacific
Coast) salt marshes; Alaska to Newfoundland and
the southernmost states.

Stems knee-high to as
high as a man, triangular
in cross section, long-
tapering to a sharp tip
above the spikelets.
Spikelets reddish-brown
to dark-red, sharp-tipped.
Ripe seeds brownish-gray.

Resembles Olney Three-
square, but the stems of
that species are 3-winged
in cross section and
short above the spikelets.
Resembles Torrey Three-
square; but the stems of
that species narrow only
a little to a round tip,
and the spikelets are
light-brown.

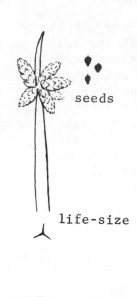

seeds

life-size

OLNEY THREESQUARE,
Scirpus olneyi

Coastal brackish
marshes and inland
alkali marshes; Wash-
ington to Wyoming,
California, and
Texas; Nova Scotia to
Louisiana.

Stems knee-high to
higher than a man,
3-winged in cross
section, the part
above the spikelets
usually not longer
than the length of
the spikelet cluster.
Spikelets brown,
blunt-tipped. Ripe
seeds brownish-gray.

Resembles Common
Threesquare; but the
stems of that species
are triangular in
cross section and
long-tapering above
the spikelets.

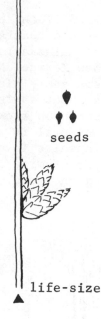

seeds

life-size ▲

TORREY THREESQUARE,
Scirpus torreyi

Inland fresh
marshes; Manitoba
to New Brunswick,
South Dakota, Mis-
souri, and New
Jersey.

Stems knee-high
to waist-high,
triangular in cross
section, narrowing
only a little above
the spikelets to a
round tip. Spike-
lets light-brown,
sharp-tipped.
Ripe seeds brown.

Resembles Common
Threesquare; but
the stems of that
species taper to a
sharp tip above the
spikelets, and the
spikelets are
usually reddish.

12

RICEFIELD BULRUSH,
Scirpus mucronatus

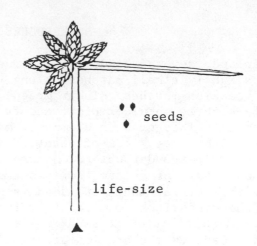

seeds

life-size

Rice fields in the Sacramento
Valley, California.
   Stems knee-high to waist-high,
in clumps, sharply triangular in
cross section, the part above
the spikelets often growing
sideways. Spikelets greenish,
their scales edged with brown.
Ripe seeds black.

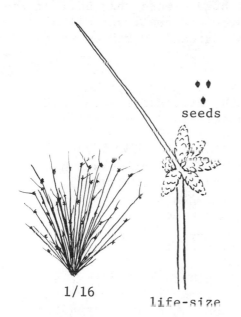

seeds

1/16

life-size

BLUNTSCALE BULRUSH,
Scirpus smithii
(Scirpus debilis and purshianus)

Inland and occasionally coastal
fresh marshes; Minnesota to Quebec,
Alabama, and Georgia.
   Stems ankle-high to knee-high,
in clumps, bluntly triangular to
round in cross section, the part
above the spikelets often growing
sideways. Spikelets greenish to
light-brown. Ripe seeds black.

RUSH FUIRENA, Fuirena scirpoidea
(Fuirena longa)

Inland fresh marshes; Texas to
Florida and southern Georgia.
   Stems less than knee-high to
waist-high, with loose, usually
bladeless leaf sheaths. Spikelets dark-brown. Ripe seeds
dark-brown.

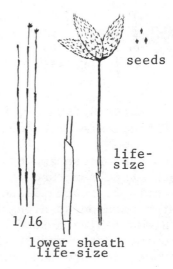

seeds

life-
size

1/16

lower sheath
life-size

13

SPIKERUSHES, Eleocharis

Inland, several kinds of Spikerush grow in fresh, slightly brackish, and slightly alkali marshes; along the coasts, several grow in fresh and brackish marshes. Their green, leafless stems vary from less than ankle-high to shoulder-high, and from as thin as thread to as thick as a pencil. They grow in clumps or make a turf, either in colonies or mixed with other kinds of plants. Slender, Dwarf, and Water Spikerushes are sometimes under water. Mature stems are tipped with a single lance-shaped, oval, or oblong, scaly spikelet which is yellowish, brown, reddish, or blackish. One seed is produced under each scale.

Some kinds look so much alike that they can be told apart only by using magnification to study their seeds and the tubercle which caps a seed. Besides the species described here, there are about 30 others which grow along the landward edge of marshes, in damp meadows, on the shores of lakes, ponds, and streams, or in bogs. More than half of the North American species are described in Gray's Manual; and all of them by Henry Svenson in the New York Botanical Garden's North American Flora, volume 18, part 9.

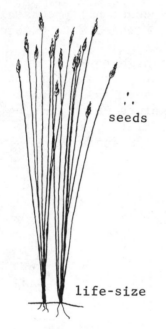

seeds

life-size

SLENDER SPIKERUSH, Eleocharis acicularis
(Eleocharis bella and radicans)

Inland fresh marshes; Far North to the southernmost States (commonest in southeastern Canada and northeastern United States).
Stems usually making a turf no more than ankle high; sometimes under water with limp stems up to a foot long. Spikelets oval or lance-shaped, usually whitish-and-red-streaked. Ripe seeds whitish.
Resembles Dwarf Spikerush; but that species usually has thicker stems and tiny underground tubers and is common in brackish Atlantic Coast marshes.

DWARF SPIKERUSH, Eleocharis parvula
(Eleocharis coloradoensis, Scirpus nanus)

Coastal fresh and brackish marshes and inland fresh, brackish, and alkali marshes; British Columbia to Newfoundland and the southernmost States (commonest along the Atlantic Coast).
Stems making a turf no more than ankle-high; sometimes under water. In summer and fall has tiny underground tubers. Spikelets oval, greenish or brown. Ripe seeds yellowish or brown.
Resembles Slender Spikerush (see above).

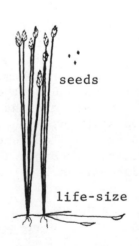

seeds

life-size

TRIANGLESTEM SPIKERUSH,
Eleocharis robbinsii

Inland fresh marshes; Minnesota to Nova Scotia and Florida.

Stems ankle-high to less than waist-high, triangular in cross section; sometimes with additional threadlike underwater stems. Spikelets lance-shaped, greenish. Ripe seeds brown.

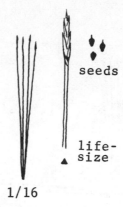

seeds

life-size

1/16

WATER SPIKERUSH,
Eleocharis elongata

Inland fresh marshes and water; Louisiana to Florida and southern Georgia.

Stems usually under water, threadlike, to 3 feet long, and flowerless; a few thicker stems, with spikelets, reaching a little out of water. Spikelets lance-shaped, green-and-brown-streaked. Ripe seeds light-brown.

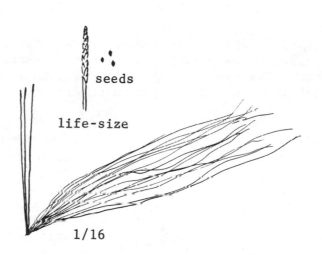

seeds

life-size

1/16

COMMON SPIKERUSH, Eleocharis palustris
(Eleocharis ambigens, calva, fallax, halophila, macrostachya, smallii, and uniglumis)

Inland fresh and alkali marshes and coastal fresh and brackish marshes; Alaska to Labrador and the southernmost States (commonest in southern Canada and the northern half of United States).

Stems ankle-high to shoulder-high. Spikelets lance-shaped or rarely oval, yellowish, brown, reddish-streaked, or dark-red. Ripe seeds yellowish to dark-brown, biconvex in end view.

Medium-sized plants resemble Walking Spikerush, but that species often has long, sideways-growing stems which root at the tip, and greenish-brown seeds which are triangular in end view.

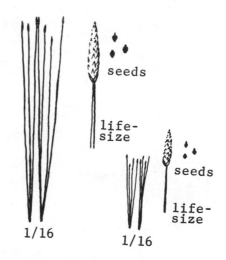

seeds

life-size

seeds

life-size

1/16

1/16

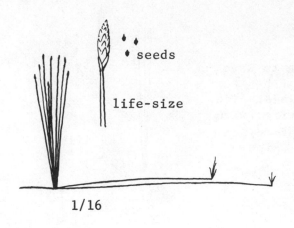

seeds

life-size

1/16

WALKING SPIKERUSH, Eleocharis rostellata

Inland alkali and fresh marshes; British Columbia to Alberta, California, and Texas; Minnesota to Nova Scotia and Florida (rare in the southeastern States).

Stems more than ankle-high to waist-high, usually in clumps, often with long sideways-growing stems which root at the tip. Spikelets lance-shaped or oval, yellowish or brown. Ripe seeds greenish-brown, triangular in end view.

Resembles medium-sized Common Spikerush; but that species does not have sideways-growing stems which root at the tip, and it has yellowish to dark-brown seeds which are biconvex in end view.

BLUNT SPIKERUSH, Eleocharis obtusa (Eleocharis diandra, engelmanni, macounii, and ovata)

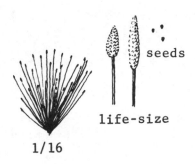

seeds

life-size

1/16

Inland fresh marshes; British Columbia to Newfoundland and the southernmost States (commonest in the eastern half of the United States).

Stems ankle-high to knee-high, in big clumps. Spikelets oval or oblong, brown. Ripe seeds brown, biconvex in end view.

Plants with shot spikelets resembling Saltmarsh Spikerush; but that species grows in Atlantic-Coast brackish marshes and has yellowish spikelets, and its seeds are triangular in end view.

SALTMARSH SPIKERUSH, Eleocharis albida

seeds

life-size

1/16

Coastal brackish marshes; Delaware to Texas.

Stems ankle-high to less than knee-high, in clumps. Spikelets oval or oblong, yellowish. Ripe seeds brown, triangular in end view.

Resembles plants of Blunt Spikerush with short spikelets, but that species grows in inland fresh marshes and has brown spikelets, and its seeds are biconvex in end view.

SQUARESTEM SPIKERUSH,
Eleocharis quadrangulata

Inland and coastal fresh marshes;
California; Wisconsin to Massachusetts,
Texas, and Florida.
Stems knee-high to waist-high, squarish
or rarely triangular in cross section.
Spikelets linear-oblong, yellowish. Ripe
seeds brown.

NORTHERN JOINTED SPIKERUSH,
Eleocharis equisetoides

Inland fresh marshes; Wisconsin to
Massachusetts, Texas, and Florida (commonest in the Southeast).
Stems knee-high to waist-high, round
in cross section, with cross partitions
about the same distance apart (split a
stem lengthwise to make sure). Spikelets and seeds resembling those of
Squarestem Spikerush.
Resembles Southern Jointed Spikerush;
but the stems of that species have cross
partitions much closer to each other just
below a spikelet than farther down.
Resembles Gulf Spikerush; but the stems
of that species do not have partitions.

SOUTHERN JOINTED SPIKERUSH,
Eleocharis interstincta

Inland fresh marshes; Texas and Florida.
Resembles Northern Jointed Spikerush,
except that the cross partitions in a stem
are much closer to each other just below
a spikelet than farther down.

GULF SPIKERUSH, Eleocharis cellulosa

Coastal fresh and brackish marshes, and
rarely inland fresh marshes; Texas to
Florida and North Carolina.
Stems less than knee-high to less than
waist-high, round or rarely triangular in
cross section. Spikelets and seeds resembling those of Squarestem Spikerush.
Resembles the Jointed Spikerushes; but
the stems of those species have partitions.

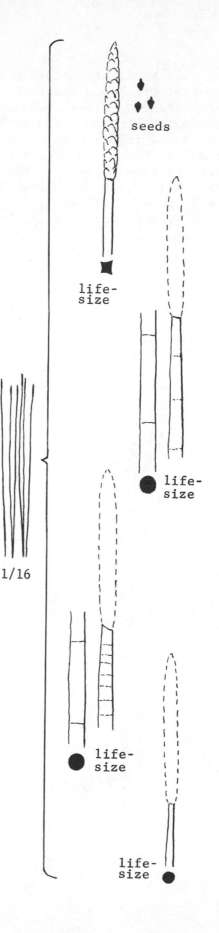

seeds

life-
size

1/16

life-
size

life-
size

life-
size

17

CATTAILS, Typha

Four kinds of Cattail grow in inland fresh and alkali marshes and coastal fresh and brackish marshes from Alaska to Newfoundland and the southernmost States, usually as dense colonies of upright leaves which are waist-high to twice as high as a man. Among the leaves in summer are stems topped with brown seed spikes from an inch or two long in the smallest Narrowleaf Cattail to a foot and a half in the biggest South-ern and Blue Cattails. Early in a growing season, these spikes are in two parts: a soft yellowish mass of male flowers above and a firm green or brown mass of female flowers below. The male flowers soon fall and leave a bare, gray, slightly rough piece of stem; the female flowers develop into a thick long-lasting spike of innumerable closely packed hair-surrounded seeds.

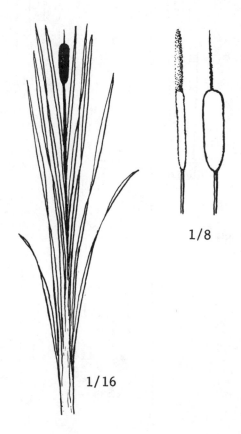

1/8

1/16

BROADLEAF CATTAIL, Typha latifolia

Alaska to Newfoundland and the southernmost States.

Leaves waist-high to higher than a man, 1/2 inch to nearly an inch wide. Spike-topped stems about the height of the leaves. Male and young green female spikes usually touching each other. When a female spike is mature and dark-greenish-brown to reddish-brown, the bare stem just above it is gray and slightly rough, not green and smooth as in the other Cattails.

NARROWLEAF CATTAIL, Typha angustifolia
(part of Typha angustifolia in Small's Manual)

Washington to Nova Scotia and the southernmost States (commonest in the northeastern quarter of United States).

Leaves usually shorter than a man and no wider than a pencil. Spike-topped stems shorter than the leaves. Male and young dark-brown female spikes usually separated by a green, smooth piece of stem several times as long as a spike is thick. Mature dark-brown female spikes not as thick as this green piece of stem is long. Above the green, the stem is gray and slightly rough.

1/8

SOUTHERN CATTAIL, Typha domingensis
(part of Typha angustifolia in Small's Manual)

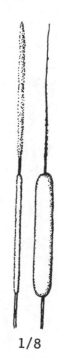

California to Delaware and the southernmost States (only along or near the coast east of the Great Plains).

Leaves as high as a man to twice as high and to about 1/2 inch wide. Spike-topped stems about the height of the leaves. Male and young light-brown female spikes usually separated by a green, smooth piece of stem 2 or 3 times as long as a spike is thick. Mature light-brown female spikes about as thick as this green piece of stem is long. Above the green, the stem is gray and slightly rough.

1/8

BLUE CATTAIL, Typha glauca

Not pictured.

Washington to Maine and the southernmost States (commonest in central New York and along Delaware and Chesapeake Bays).

Resembles Southern Cattail, except that mature female spikes are reddish-brown.

BURREEDS, Sparganium

Burreeds grow in fresh marshes and water, usually inland. Early leaves are usually under water. Mature leaves stand ankle-high to shoulder-high, or they sprawl or float. Leaves are less than an inch wide; and out-of-water ones are usually triangular in cross section. Half-hidden among the leaves are stems which toward their end have a few round, tight clusters of flowers. The upper clusters are male flowers, which soon wither. The lower clusters are female flowers, which become hard balls of seeds. These balls are on short or long stalks, or are stalkless. Ripe seeds are greenish or brown. Without the seeds it is hard to identify most kinds.

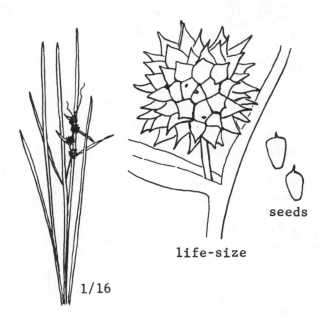

seeds

life-size

1/16

BIG BURREED,
Sparganium eurycarpum

Inland and coastal fresh marshes; British Columbia to Nova Scotia, California, Kansas, and Virginia.
Mature leaves knee-high to shoulder-high. Ripe seeds wedge-shaped below a spiny tip.

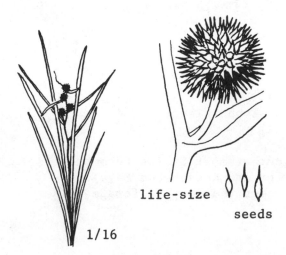

life-size

seeds

1/16

EASTERN BURREED,
Sparganium americanum

Inland fresh marshes; Minnesota to Newfoundland, Texas, and Florida.
Mature leaves to waist-high, or sometimes floating. Seed balls 1/2 inch to 1 inch in diameter, each one usually attached to the stem at the base of a leaf. Ripe seeds rather dull, tapering into a spiny tip; the main part of a seed 3/16 to 1/4 inch long.

SHINING BURREED, Sparganium androcladum

Not pictured.
Inland fresh marshes; Minnesota to Quebec, Oklahoma, and Virginia.
Mature leaves knee-high to waist-high. Seed balls similar to Eastern Burreed, except more than an inch thick. Ripe seeds also similar, except rather shiny and with the main part about 5/16 inch long.

SLENDER BURREED, Sparganium simplex
(Sparganium angustifolium, chlorocarpum, and multipedunculatum)

Not pictured.
Inland fresh marshes and water; Alaska to Labrador, California, New Mexico, and North Carolina.
Mature leaves to waist-high, or floating. Seed balls similar to Eastern Burreed, except usually attached to the stem well above the base of a leaf. Ripe seeds also similar, except rather shiny.

FLOATING BURREED, Sparganium fluctuans

Inland fresh water; British Columbia to Saskatchewan and Idaho; Minnesota to Newfoundland and Pennsylvania.
Mature leaves floating. Flower clusters usually branched. Seed balls a little smaller than Eastern Burreed, and seeds a little fatter and usually with a much-curved tip.

life-size

LITTLE BURREED, Sparganium minimum
(Sparganium hyperboreum)

Inland fresh marshes; Alaska to Greenland, New Mexico, and New Jersey.
Mature leaves sprawling or floating. Seed balls less than 1/2 inch through. Ripe seeds blunt or with a spiny tip which is less than 1/16 inch long.

life-size

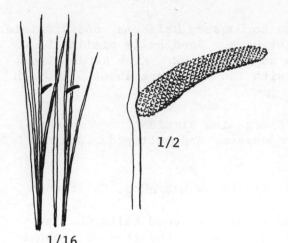

1/16

1/2

SWEETFLAG, Acorus calamus

Inland and coastal fresh
marshes; Northwest Territories
to Nova Scotia, California,
Colorado, Texas, and Florida
(commonest in the northeastern
quarter of United States).
Leaves waist-high to as high
as a man, up to an inch wide,
tapering to a sharp tip, the
main vein nearer one edge than
the other and equally conspicuous on each side. Flower
spikes yellowish-brown.
Leaves, stems, and rootstocks
spicy-scented when crushed.

1/4

SWAMP-LILY,
Crinum americanum

Inland fresh
marshes; Texas to
Florida.
Stems to less than
waist-high. Leaves
to 4 feet long and 1
3/4 inches wide.
Flowers white, fra-
grant. Seed pods
irregularly globular
1 1/2 to 2 1/2 inches
thick.

Group 2. <u>PLANTS WITH UPRIGHT OR UPSLANTED STEMS WITH GRASSLIKE
LEAVES ON TWO SIDES (ONE PLANE); FLOWERS INDIVIDUALLY INCONSPICUOUS
BETWEEN SCALES WHICH OVERLAP IN TWO ROWS TO FORM SPIKELETS, THE SPIKE-
LETS CLUSTERED TOWARD THE TOP OF STEMS</u>; growing inland in fresh and
moderately alkali marshes and along the coasts in fresh to salt marshes.
Stems usually stand so close to each other in colonies that their
leaves interlace. Most kinds come up year after year from rootstocks,
but a few grow each year from seed. They vary from no more than ankle-
high in Low Mannagrass and Coast Dropseed to three times as high as a
man in Phragmites. Flowers are in greenish, yellowish, brown, or
purplish spikelets which sometimes are in showy clusters.

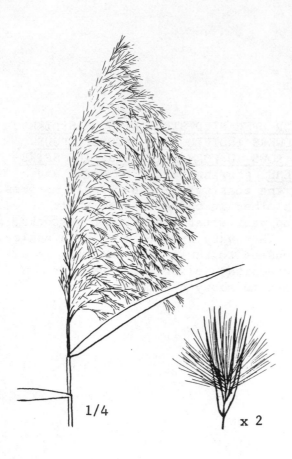

PHRAGMITES,
Phragmites communis
(Phragmites phragmites)

Inland fresh marshes and coastal fresh and brackish marshes; Northwest Territories to Nova Scotia and the southernmost States.

Stems from usually higher than a man to three times as high. Leaves grayish-green, close to each other and usually sticking out from stems at a big angle, to 2 feet long and 2 inches wide. Flower clusters to 1 1/2 feet long, often purple when young, usually whitish and fluffy when old. Each spikelet with 3 to 7 flowers, and with many long hairs on the axis between flowers.

1/4

x 2

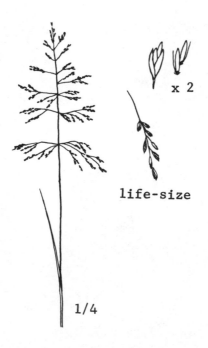

TUFTED HAIRGRASS,
Deschampsia cespitosa
(Aira caespitosa)

Coastal fresh and brackish marshes; Alaska to California. Inland, usually in less-wet places; Alaska to Baffin Island, California, New Mexico, South Dakota, and North Carolina.

Stems knee-high to shoulder-high, in clumps with leaves which are to 2 feet long. Flower clusters to a foot long. Each spikelet with 2 flowers. Flower scales with a tiny bristle attached to the back just above its base.

x 2

life-size

1/4

life-size

1/4

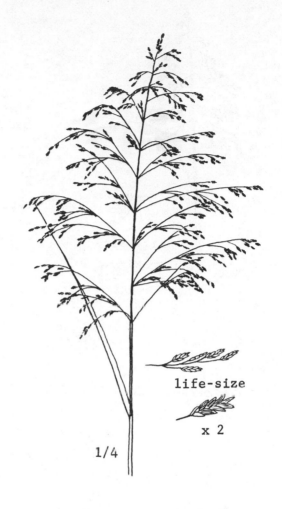

life-size

x 2

1/4

WHITETOP,
Scolochloa festucacea

　　Inland fresh marshes;
Northwest Territories to
Oregon and Iowa.
　　Stems waist-high to as
high as a man.　Leaves to
1 1/2 feet long and 3/8
inch wide.　Flower clus-
ters to a foot long.
Each spikelet with 3 or
4 flowers.

REED MANNAGRASS,
Glyceria grandis
(Panicularia grandis)

　　Inland fresh marshes;
Alaska to Newfoundland, Nevada,
New Mexico, Iowa, and Virginia.
　　Stems waist-high to as high
as a man.　Leaves to 1 1/2 feet
long and 1/2 inch wide.　Flower
clusters to 1 1/4 feet long,
usually purplish.　Each spikelet with 4 to 8 flowers.

life-size

x 2

1/4

WESTERN MANNAGRASS, Glyceria pauciflora

Inland fresh marshes; Alaska to South Dakota, California, and New Mexico.

Stems less than knee-high to more than waist-high. Leaves to 10 inches long and 5/8 inch wide. Flower clusters to 8 inches long, green or purplish. Each spikelet with 4 to 10 flowers.

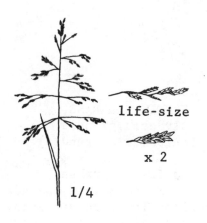

life-size

x 2

1/4

LOW MANNAGRASS, Glyceria pallida (Glyceria fernaldii, Panicularia pallida)

Inland fresh marshes; British Columbia to Newfoundland, Wyoming, Missouri, and North Carolina.

Stems from almost horizontal to waist-high. Leaves to 8 inches long and 3/8 inch wide. Flower clusters to 8 inches long, green. Eack spikelet with 3 to 7 flowers.

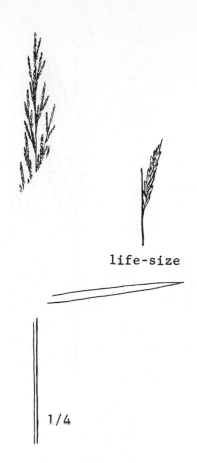

life-size

1/4

1/4

life-size

WATER MANNAGRASS,
Glyceria fluitans
(Glyceria arkansana, borealis,
leptostachya, occidentalis,
and septentrionalis; Panicularia septentrionalis)

Inland fresh marshes; Alaska
to Newfoundland, California,
Texas, and Georgia.
Stems knee-high to shoulder-
high. Leaves to a foot long
and 3/4 inch wide. Flower
clusters to 2 feet long, their
branches sometimes horizontal
when coming into bloom. Each
spikelet with 6 to 15 flowers.

SHARPSCALE MANNAGRASS,
Glyceria acutiflora
(Panicularia acutiflora)

Inland fresh marshes;
Michigan to New Hampshire,
Missouri, and Georgia.
Stems less than knee-
high to waist-high. Leaves
to 8 inches long and 1/4
inch wide. Flower clusters
to 1 1/4 feet long. Each
spikelet with 5 to 12
flowers. Flower scales
with tapering tips--unlike
other Mannagrasses.

27

BEARDED SPRANGLETOP,
Leptochloa fascicularis
(Diplachne acuminata, fascicularis,
and maritima)

Inland fresh and alkali marshes and coastal brackish and fresh marshes; Washington to New Hampshire and the southernmost States (rare inland east of Mississippi River).

Stems less than knee-high to waist-high. Leaves to 1 1/2 feet long and 3/16 inch wide, often overtopping the flower clusters. Eack spikelet with 6 to 12 flowers.

life-size

x 2

1/4

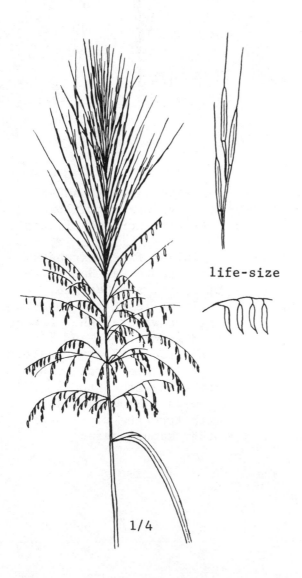

life-size

1/4

WILDRICE, Zizania aquatica

Inland and coastal fresh marshes; Manitoba to Nova Scotia, Texas, and Florida (only close to the coast in the southeastern States). Rarely established from planting; Washington to Alberta and California.

Stems waist-high to twice as high as a man. Leaves to 4 feet long and 2 inches wide, with very rough edges. Flower clusters to 2 feet long, their lower branches with dangling short-lived male spikelets, their upper branches with upright one-flowered female spikelets. The scales of matured female flowers tightly enclose a long, narrow seed.

28

GIANT CUTGRASS,
Zizaniopsis miliacea

Inland and coastal fresh
marshes; Illinois to Maryland,
Texas, and Florida.
Stems waist-high to twice as
high as a man. Leaves to 4
feet long and 1 1/2 inches
wide, with very rough edges.
Flower clusters to 2 feet
long, their widely spreading or
drooping branches with separate
but similar-looking, one-
flowered male and female spikelets on the same branch. The
scales of matured female
flowers are loose around an
oval seed.

life-size

1/4

RICE, Oryza sativa

Cultivated as a marsh plant;
California; Missouri to South
Carolina, Texas, and Louisiana.
Stems waist-high to as high
as a man. Leaves to 1 1/2
feet long and 1/2 inch wide.
Flower clusters to 1 1/2
feet long, usually with drooping branches. Spikelets one-
flowered, flattish, their
scales rough to touch, sometimes tipped with a bristle.

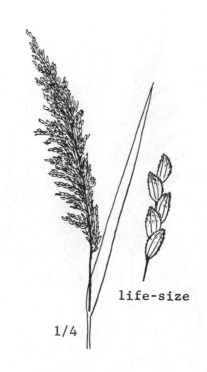

life-size

1/4

29

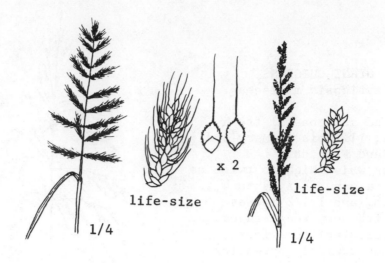

life-size

x 2

life-size

1/4

1/4

WILD MILLET, Echinochloa crusgalli
(Echinochloa pungens)

Inland and coastal fresh marshes and less-wet places; British Columbia to Prince Edward Island and the southernmost States.

Stems knee-high to as high as a man. Leaves to 1 1/2 feet long and 1 inch wide. Leaf sheaths hairless. Flower clusters to 1 1/2 feet long, green to purple, loose to dense. Spikelets one-flowered, fine-hairy, with or without bristle tips.

A form which has dense clusters of bristle-tipped spikelets resembles Walter Millet; but the lower leaf sheaths of that species are usually hairy and the bristle tips of its spikelets are longer.

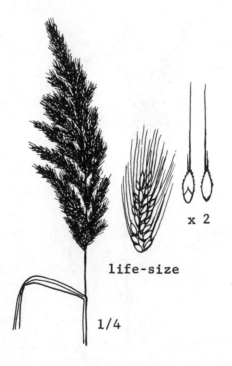

x 2

life-size

1/4

WALTER MILLET, Echinochloa walteri

Inland fresh marshes and coastal fresh and brackish marshes; Minnesota to Quebec, Texas, and Florida.

Stems waist-high to higher than a man. Leaves to 1 1/2 feet long and 1 inch wide. Lower leaf sheaths usually coarse-hairy. Flower clusters to 1 1/2 feet long, green or purplish, usually dense. Spikelets one-flowered, fine-hairy, with bristle tips to 1 1/2 inches long.

Resembles a form of Wild Millet which has dense clusters of bristle-tipped spikelets; but that species has hairless leaf sheaths, and the bristle tips of its spikelets are usually shorter.

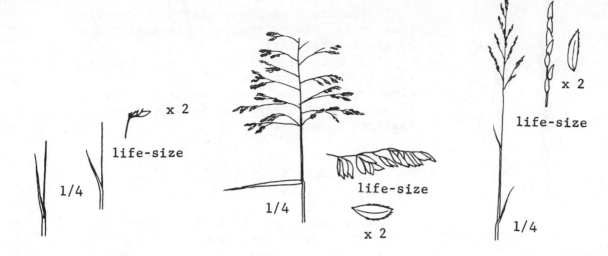

REED CANARYGRASS, Phalaris arundinacea	RICE CUTGRASS, Leersia oryzoides (Homalocenchrus oryzoides)	SOUTHERN CUTGRASS, Leersia hexandra (Homalocenchrus hexandrus)

REED CANARYGRASS, Phalaris arundinacea

Inland fresh marshes and less-wet places; Alaska to Newfoundland, California, New Mexico, and North Carolina.

Stems knee-high to as high as a man. Leaves to a foot long and 3/4 inch wide, grayish-green. Flower clusters to 8 inches long, usually standing high above leaves, rather open when coming into bloom. Spikelets one-flowered. Scales of matured flowers leathery and tight around a seed.

RICE CUTGRASS, Leersia oryzoides (Homalocenchrus oryzoides)

Inland and coastal fresh marshes; British Columbia to Nova Scotia and the southern-most States (commoner in eastern half of this range).

Stems knee-high to shoulder-high. Leaves to 10 inches long and 1/2 inch wide, their blades and sheaths usually so rough that they abrade skin and clothing. Flower clusters to 8 inches long. Spikelets one-flowered, flattish, blunt-tipped.

SOUTHERN CUTGRASS, Leersia hexandra (Homalocenchrus hexandrus)

Inland fresh marshes; Texas to Virginia and Florida.

Stems ankle-high to waist-high. Leaves to 10 inches long and 1/4 inch wide, their blades and sheaths not as rough as Rice Cutgrass. Flower clusters to 4 inches long. Spikelets one-flowered, flattish, sharp-tipped.

Resembles Rice Cutgrass; but the flower clusters of that species are wider and the flower scales are blunter.

SLOUGHGRASS, Beckmannia syzigachne

Inland fresh marshes; Alaska to Ontario, California, New Mexico, and Wisconsin, and rarely farther east.

Stems knee-high to waist-high. Leaves to a foot long and 1/2 inch wide. Flower clusters to a foot long. Spikelets one-flowered, almost circular in side view, flattish in end view.

life-size x 2

1/4

SALTGRASS, Distichlis spicata
(Distichlis stricta)

Coastal salt and brackish marshes; British Columbia to California; Nova Scotia to Texas. Inland alkali marshes; British Columbia to Manitoba, California, and Texas.

Stems ankle-high to knee-high. Leaves to 6 inches long and 1/8 inch wide, usually close to each other and standing out from the stem at a wide angle. Flower clusters to 3 inches long. Male spikelets are as much as an inch long and have as many as 20 flowers. Female spikelets are on separate plants, and are shorter and have fewer flowers.

Stems and leaves resemble those of Coast Dropseed.

1/4

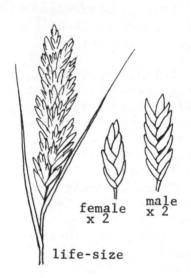

female x 2   male x 2

life-size

COAST DROPSEED, Sporobolus virginicus

Coastal salt marshes; Texas to North Carolina.

Stems ankle-high to knee-high. Leaves to 4 inches long and 1/8 inch wide, usually close to each other and standing out from the stem at a wide angle. Flower clusters to 3 inches long. Spikelets one-flowered.

Stems and leaves resemble those of Saltgrass.

x 2

life-size

1/4

GIANT SETARIA, Setaria magna
(Chaetochloa magna)

Coastal and rarely inland brackish
and fresh marshes; Texas to New Jersey
and Florida.

Stems waist-high to twice as high
as a man. Leaves to 2 feet long and
1 1/2 inches wide. Flower clusters
to 2 feet long. Spikelets one-
flowered, crowded among long
bristles.

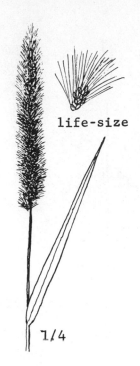

life-size

1/4

SACCIOLEPIS, Sacciolepis striata

Inland fresh marshes; Oklahoma to
Delaware, Texas, and Florida.

Stems less than knee-high to as high
as a man. Leaves to 10 inches long and
3/4 inch wide. Flower clusters to a
foot long. Spikelets one-flowered,
on tiny stalks, dropping early.

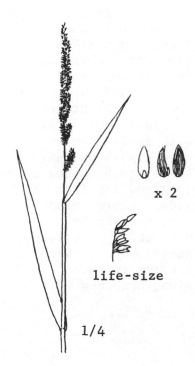

x 2

life-size

1/4

33

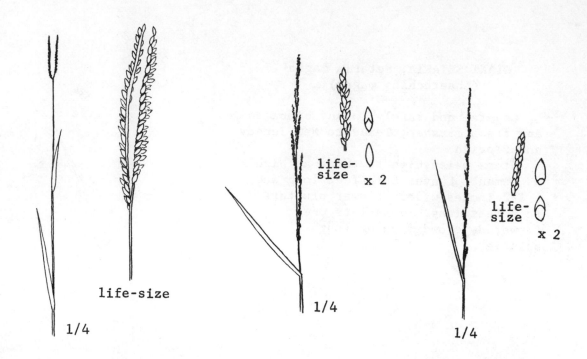

life-size

1/4

life-
size   x 2

1/4

life-
size

x 2

1/4

JOINTGRASS,
Paspalum distichum
(Paspalum vaginatum)

Inland fresh
marshes and coastal
fresh and brackish
marshes; Washington
to Oklahoma, New
Jersey, and the
southernmost States.
Stems horizontal,
with ankle-high to
knee-high branches.
Leaves to 6 inches
long and 1/4 inch
wide. Flower clus-
ters usually 2-
branched. Spikelets
one-flowered, over-
lapping in rows
along branches.

MAIDENCANE,
Panicum hemitomon

Inland and coastal
fresh marshes; Texas
to New Jersey and
Florida.
Stems knee-high to
as high as a man,
often with their
bases in a foot or
two of water. Leaves
to a foot long and
3/4 inch wide.
Flower clusters to a
foot long, their
upper branches much
shorter than the
lower and much more
overlapping. Spike-
lets one-flowered,
irregularly clus-
tered along branches.

WATER PANICUM,
Panicum paludivagum

Inland fresh
marshes; South Caro-
lina, Texas, and
Florida.
Lower part of stems
usually horizontal and
under water, upper
part vertical and as
much as waist-high
above water. Leaves
to a foot long and 1/4
inch wide. Flower
clusters to a foot
long, their upper
branches only a little
shorter than the lower
and a little more
overlapping. Spike-
lets one-flowered,
overlapping in rows
along branches.

PRAIRIE CORDGRASS,
Spartina pectinata
(Spartina michauxiana)

Inland fresh marshes and less-wet places, and coastal fresh and brackish marshes; Saskatchewan to Newfoundland Washington, Texas, and North Carolina.

Stems waist-high to as high as a man. Leaves to 4 feet long and 5/8 inch wide, very rough on the edges, tapering to a threadlike tip. Flower clusters to 1 1/2 feet long, usually with fewer than 20 branches, all about the same length. Spikelets one-flowered, flattish. The two lower scales of each spikelet usually bristle-tipped.

Along the coast between Massachusetts and North Carolina, sometimes grows near and resembles Big Cordgrass; but the flower clusters of that species usually have more branches, and the branches at the top of its clusters are usually much shorter than those at the bottom.

1/4   life-size   x 2

BIG CORDGRASS,
Spartina cynosuroides

Coastal brackish marshes; Massachusetts to Florida and Texas.

Stems waist-high to half again as high as a man. Leaves to an inch wide. Flower clusters to 1 1/2 feet long, usually with more than 30 branches and with the branches at the top of a cluster usually much shorter than those at the bottom. Spikelets similar to Prairie Cordgrass, except that none of the scales are bristle-tipped.

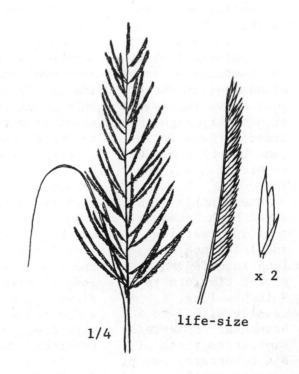

1/4   life-size   x 2

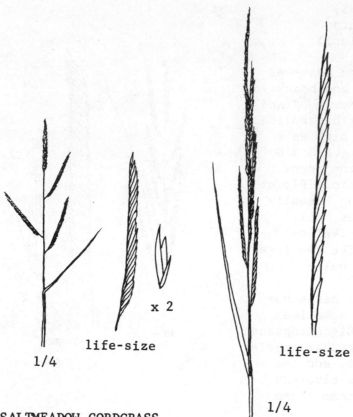

x 2

life-size

1/4

SALTMEADOW CORDGRASS,
Spartina patens

Coastal brackish
marshes; Newfoundland
to Florida and Texas
(the principal plant
on thousands of acres
of meadowlike marsh
just above the level
of ordinary high
tides). Rare in in-
land brackish marshes
in Michigan and New
York.

Stems ankle-high to
waist-high. Leaves
to 1 1/2 feet long
and 1/16 inch wide,
long-tapering.
Flower clusters to
8 inches long,
usually with 3 to 6
branches. Spikelets
similar to those of
Big Cordgrass, except
usually smaller.

life-size

1/4

SALTMARSH CORDGRASS,
Spartina alterniflora

Coastal salt
marshes; Washington;
Newfoundland to Flor-
ida and Texas (the
only plant on thou-
sands of acres next
to the Atlantic).

Stems from ankle-
high where the ground
is barely flooded by
high tides to higher
than a man along
marsh creeks. Leaves
to 1 1/2 feet long
and 3/4 inch wide,
long-tapering.
Flower clusters to
a foot long, usually
with long, upright
branches. Spikelets
similar to those of
Big Cordgrass.

life-size

1/4

CALIFORNIA CORDGRASS,
Spartina foliosa

Coastal salt
marshes, where the
ground is shallowly
flooded by high tides;
California.

Stems less than
knee-high to shoulder-
high. Leaves to 1 1/2
feet long and 1/2 inch
wide, long-tapering.
Flower clusters to 10
inches long, usually
with short, upright
branches. Spikelets
similar to those of
Big Cordgrass.

36

Group 3. <u>PLANTS WITH UPRIGHT STEMS WITH GRASSLIKE LEAVES ON THREE</u>
<u>SIDES; FLOWERS INDIVIDUALLY INCONSPICUOUS BETWEEN SCALES WHICH USUALLY</u>
<u>OVERLAP IN SEVERAL ROWS TO FORM SPIKELETS, THE SPIKELETS CLUSTERED</u>
<u>TOWARD THE TOP OF STEMS</u>; growing inland in fresh and alkali marshes and
along the coasts in fresh to brackish marshes. Stems usually stand so
close to each other in colonies that their leaves interlace. Most
kinds come up year after year from rootstocks. They vary from ankle-
high in Redroot Cyperus to half again as high as a man in Sawgrass.
Redroot Cyperus grows from seed each year, and is the only one of the
group which has spikelet scales overlapping in only two rows. Flowers
are in greenish, yellowish, brown, or blackish spikelets which are not
very showy, even when clustered.

SEDGES, Carex

Inland, several kinds of Sedge grow in fresh marshes; along the coasts, several grow in fresh, brackish, and salt marshes. Their leafy stems, single or in clumps, vary from less than ankle-high to shoulder-high. Toward the top they bear upright to dangling spikelets of closely packed, individually inconspicuous flowers which are partly hidden by greenish, yellowish, brown, purplish, or blackish scales. Some kinds have male and female flowers in different parts of each spikelet; others have male flowers in spikelets at the top of stems, female flowers in different-looking spikelets farth r down.

1/4

x 2

life-size

Male flowers soon wither. Each female flower is in a sac which grows bigger and finally contains one ripe seed.

Besides the species described here, there are many which grow along the landward edge of marshes, in damp meadows, on the shores of lakes, ponds, and streams, or in bogs. Many others grow in well-drained soils. About half of the more than 500 North American species are described in Gray's Manual, and all of them by Kenneth Mackenzie in the New York Botanical Garden's North American Flora, volume 18, parts 1 to 7.

BEAKED SEDGE, Carex rostrata

Inland fresh marshes; Alaska to Newfoundland, California, New Mexico, and West Virginia.

Stems less than knee-high to waist-high, single or in small clumps, overtopped by leaves to 1/2 inch wide. Female spikelets two to five, 1/4 to 3/4 inch thick. Seed sacs roundish in end view, partly hidden under sharp-tipped to bristle-tipped scales.

38

SLOUGH SEDGE,
Carex trichocarpa
(Carex atherodes, laevicon-
ica, sheldonii, and
subimpressa)

Inland fresh marshes; Yukon to Maine, California, Missouri, and North Carolina.

Stems less than knee-high to shoulder-high, in small clumps, overtopping or overtopped by leaves to 1/2 inch wide. Female spikelets two to four, 3/8 to 5/8 inch thick. Seed sacs 1/4 to 1/2 inch long, hairless or fine-hairy, roundish in end view, partly hidden under sharp-tipped to bristle-tipped scales.

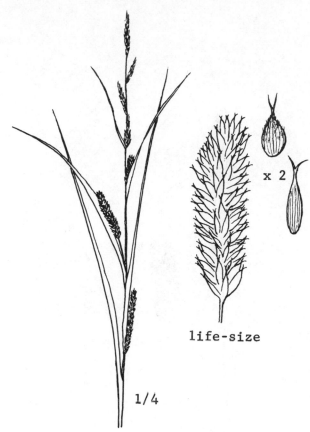

x 2

life-size

1/4

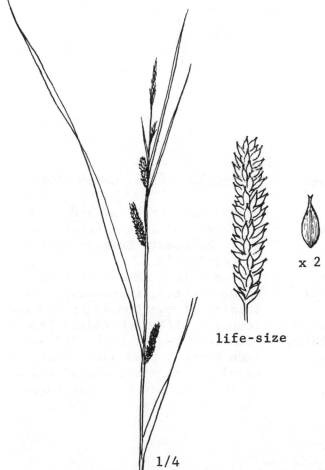

1/4

life-size

x 2

LAKE SEDGE, Carex riparia
(Carex hyalinolepis and
lacustris)

Inland and coastal fresh marshes; Alberta to Newfoundland, Texas, and Florida.

Stems knee-high to shoulder-high, in small clumps, overtopping or overtopped by leaves to 5/8 inch wide. Female spikelets two to four, 3/8 to 5/8 inch thick. Seed sacs roundish in end view, partly hidden under sharp-tipped to bristle-tipped scales.

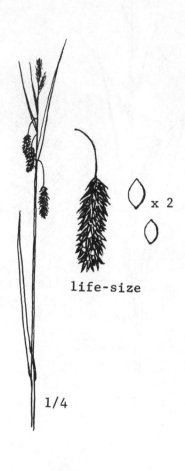

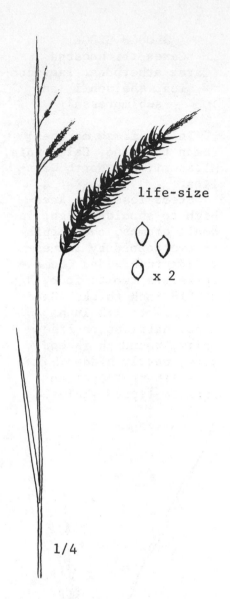

LYNGBYE SEDGE, Carex lyngbyei

   Coastal brackish and salt
marshes; Alaska to California;
Greenland to Quebec.
   Stems less than knee-high to
waist-high in clumps, overtopping leaves to 1/2 inch wide.
Female spikelets two to four,
usually dangling, 3/16 to 3/8
inch thick. Seed sacs not shiny,
two-edged in end view, partly
hidden by sharp-tipped to
bristle-tipped, brown to blackish scales.

PACIFIC SEDGE, Carex obnupta

   Coastal fresh and brackish
marshes, and inland fresh marshes
near the coast; British Columbia
to California.
   Stems less than knee-high to
shoulder-high, in clumps, overtopping or overtopped by evergreen
leaves to 1/4 inch wide. Female
spikelets two to four, 1/8 to 3/8
inch thick. Seed sacs shiny, two-
edged in end view, almost hidden
by sharp-tipped to taper-tipped,
blackish scales.

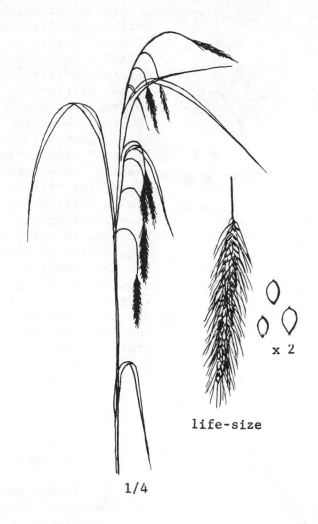

x 2

life-size

1/4

SALTMARSH SEDGE, Carex paleacea

Salt marshes; Manitoba to Newfoundland and
Massachusetts.

Stems less than knee-high to waist-high, single or
in small clumps, overtopped by leaves to 1/2 inch wide.
Female spikelets two to six, usually dangling, 3/8 to
3/4 inch thick. Seed sacs two-edged in end view, almost
hidden by long-bristle-tipped, brownish scales.

41

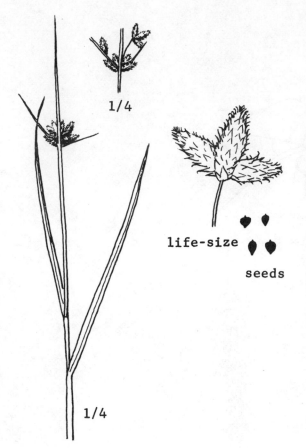

ALKALI BULRUSH, Scirpus paludosus (part of Scirpus robustus in Mason's Flora)

Coastal brackish and salt marshes; British Columbia to California; Quebec to New Jersey. Inland alkali and brackish marshes; British Columbia to Manitoba, California, and Texas; central New York.

Stems knee-high to shoulder-high. Leaves to 2 feet long and 1/2 inch wide. Mature spikelets usually straw-colored or light-brown, the bristle tips of their scales straight or curved out. Ripe seeds brown, slightly biconvex in end view.

Resembles Saltmarsh Bulrush; but that species usually has reddish-brown spikelets, the tips of its scales are recurved, and its seeds are flattish on one side and low-convex on the other in end view.

1/4

life-size

seeds

1/4

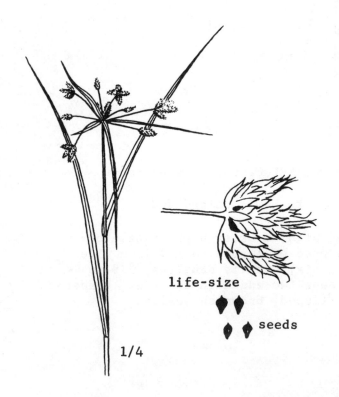

RIVER BULRUSH, Scirpus fluviatilis

Inland and coastal fresh marshes; Saskatchewan to New Brunswick, California, New Mexico, and Virginia (commonest in the north-eastern quarter of United States).

Stems waist-high to as high as a man. Flowering stems with 4 or 5 leaves. In dryish marshes, often without flowers and with a dozen or more leaves to a stem. Leaves to 2 feet long and an inch wide. Mature spikelets dull-brown. Ripe seeds greenish-brown, tri-angular in end view.

life-size

seeds

1/4

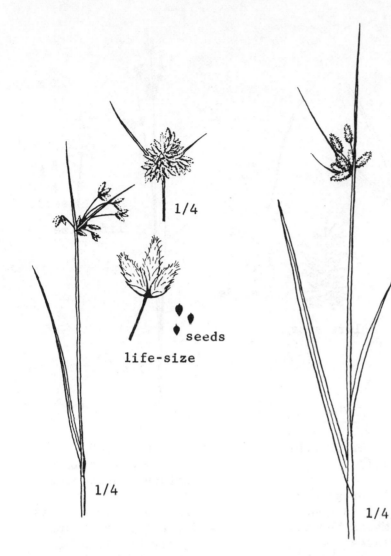

1/4

seeds

life-size

1/4

seeds

life-size

1/4

TUBEROUS BULRUSH,
Scirpus tuberosus

A native of the Old
World which has become
abundant in a few in-
land fresh to slightly
alkali marshes in Idaho
and California.

Stems knee-high to
waist-high. Leaves to
1 1/2 feet long and 1/4
inch wide. Mature spike-
lets brown, in loose or
dense clusters. Ripe
seeds brown, flattish on
one side and high-convex
on the other in end
view.

SALTMARSH BULRUSH, Scirpus robustus
(part of Scirpus robustus in
Mason's Flora)

Coastal brackish and salt marshes;
Washington; California; New Brunswick
to Texas.

Stems knee-high to shoulder-high.
Leaves to 1 1/2 feet long and 3/8
inch wide. Mature spikelets usually
reddish-brown, the bristle tips of
their scales recurved. Ripe seeds
brown, flattish on one side and low-
convex on the other in end view.

Resembles Alkali Bulrush; but that
species usually has straw-colored or
light-brown spikelets, the tips of
its scales are straight or curved
out, and its seeds are slightly
biconvex in end view.

43

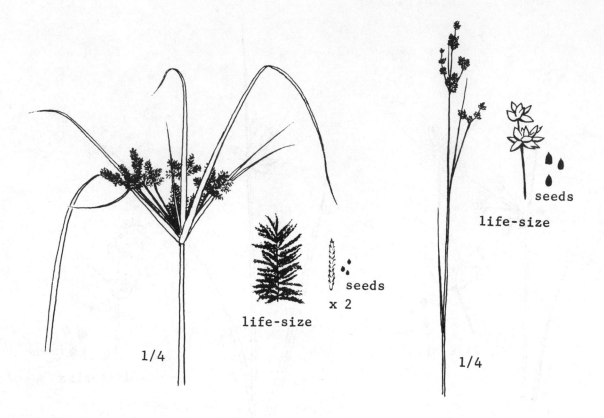

x 2

seeds

life-size

life-size

seeds

1/4

1/4

REDROOT CYPERUS, Cyperus erythrorhizos
(Cyperus halei)

Inland fresh marshes, on ground
from which standing water is gone by
summer; Washington to Massachusetts
and the southernmost States.
Stems ankle-high to waist-high,
single or in clumps, with several long
leaves toward the base and a cluster
of 4 to 10 leaves at the top. Roots
and the sheaths of lower leaves reddish. Mature spikelets reddish-brown,
1/8 to 3/4 inch long. Ripe seeds
light-brown or gray.
More than a dozen other kinds of
Cyperus grow in marshes, along the
edge of marshes, or on the shores of
lakes, ponds, and streams. Most of
them resemble Redroot Cyperus in
having a cluster of tiny-flowered
spikelets surrounded by leaves at the
top of a stem, but differ from it and
from each other in flower scales and
seeds.

TWIG-RUSH,
Cladium mariscoides
(Mariscus mariscoides)

Inland fresh marshes
and coastal fresh and
slightly brackish
marshes; Saskatchewan to
Newfoundland, Alabama,
and Florida.
Stems knee-high to
waist-high. Leaves
about the height and
width of stems. Flower
clusters to a foot long.
Mature spikelets brown.
Ripe seeds brown, round-
ish in end view.

44

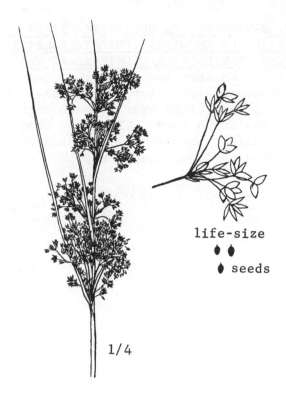

life-size

♦ ♦

♦ seeds

1/4

seeds

life-size

SAWGRASS, Cladium jamaicense
(Cladium californicum, Mariscus
jamaicensis)

   Inland and coastal fresh marshes;
California through the southern
border States to Virginia.
   Stems waist-high to half again as
high as a man. Leaves to 6 feet
long and 3/8 inch wide, their edges
very rough when rubbed downward.
Flower clusters to 3 feet long.
Mature spikelets brown. Ripe seeds
brown, roundish in end view.

EVERGLADE BEAKRUSH,
Rhynchospora tracyi

   Inland fresh marshes;
North Carolina to Florida
and Mississippi
   Stems knee-high (usually)
to waist-high. Leaves to
2 feet long and about the
width of the stems.
Mature spikelets brown.
Ripe seeds brown, flattish
in end view.

Group 4. <u>PLANTS WITH UPRIGHT, SPRAWLING, OR HORIZONTAL STEMS WITH</u>
<u>SINGLY PLACED, NON GRASSLIKE, LANCE-SHAPED OR WIDER, UNTOOTHED LEAVES</u>;
<u>FLOWERS CLUSTERED AT THE END OF STEMS OR SINGLE OR CLUSTERED AT THE</u>
<u>BASE OF LEAVES</u>; growing inland in fresh marshes and along the coasts in
fresh to salt marshes. Stems are close to each other in colonies, or
scattered. In some kinds they come up year after year from underground
or underwater stems, in others each year from seed. They vary from
sometimes floating in a few kinds to higher than a man in Tidemarsh
Waterhemp. Flowers are white, greenish, yellow, blue, or pink.

Smartweeds grow in fresh marshes and shallow water, inland and along the coasts. Most kinds have upright, branched stems with lance-shaped to oval leaves. At the end of stems are spikes of pink, white, or greenish flowers. The flowers are long-lasting and eventually enclose single brown or black seeds which are often eaten by ducks. Some kinds not described here often grow on flat land which may be covered with shallow water in winter, after the plants have died.

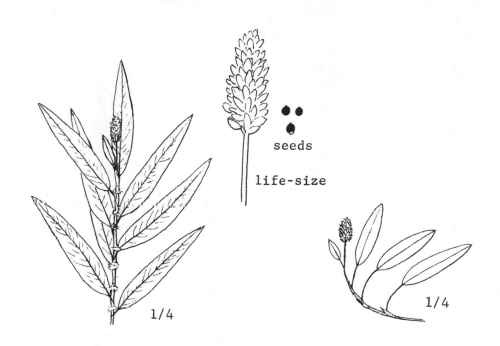

seeds

life-size

1/4

1/4

WATER SMARTWEED, Polygonum amphibium
(Polygonum natans)

Inland fresh marshes and water; Alaska to Labrador, California, New Mexico, Illinois, and Maryland.

There is a marsh form and a floating-leaved form. The marsh form has stems knee-high to waist-high; leaf blades to 6 inches long, without a narrowly tapering tip as in Marsh Smartweed; top of leaf sheaths flaring at right angles to stem; flower spikes deep-pink, oval or oblong, on a hairless stalk; ripe seeds dark-brown, thick-biconvex in end view. The floating-leaved form has shorter, blunt leaves without a flaring sheath.

The floating-leaved form resembles the floating-leaved form of Marsh Smartweed; but that species has long, narrow spikes on a fine-hairy stalk and usually has bigger leaves with a notched base.

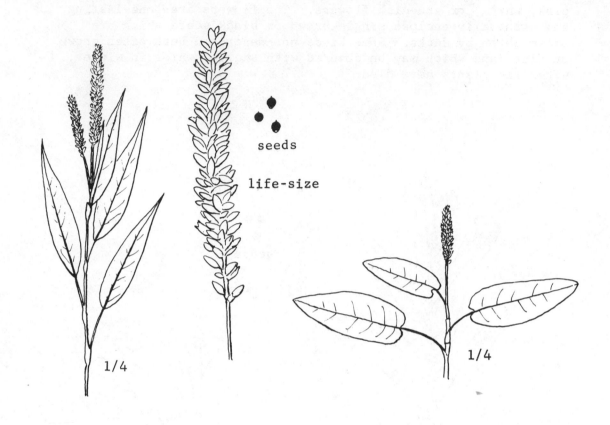

seeds

life-size

1/4

1/4

MARSH SMARTWEED, Polygonum coccineum
(Persicaria muhlenbergii)

Inland fresh marshes and water; British Columbia to Quebec, California, Texas, and South Carolina.

There is a marsh form and a floating-leaved form. The marsh form
has stems knee-high to shoulder-high; leaf blades to 8 inches long,
with a narrowly tapering tip; top of leaf sheaths not flaring; flower
spikes deep-pink, long and narrow, on a fine-hairy stalk; ripe seeds
similar to those of Water Smartweed, except larger. The floating-
leaved form has oval leaves which are usually notched at the base.

The floating-leaved form resembles the floating-leaved form of
Water Smartweed; but that species has oval or oblong spikes on a
hairless stalk and usually has smaller leaves which are not notched
at the base.

48

NODDING SMARTWEED,
Polygonum lapathifolium
   (Polygonum scabrum,
Persicaria lapathifolia)

   Inland and coastal
fresh marshes; Alaska to
Newfoundland and the
southernmost States.
   Stems knee-high to as
high as a man. Leaves
to 8 inches long.
Flowers pink, white, or
greenish in usually
curved spikes. Ripe
seeds brown to black,
flattish in end view and
usually concave on each
side.

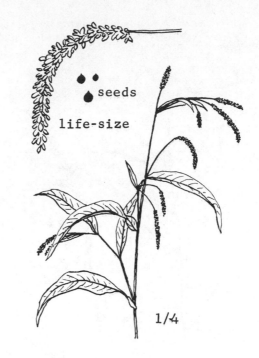

seeds

life-size

1/4

SWAMP SMARTWEED,
Polygonum hydropiperoides
(Polygonum opelousanum
and setaceum; Persicaria
hydropiperoides, opelou-
sana, paludicola, and
         setacea)

   Inland and coastal
fresh marshes; Alaska to
California; Nebraska to
Nova Scotia, Texas, and
Florida.
   Stems less than knee-
high to waist-high.
Leaves to 6 inches long.
Flowers white or pink in
straight spikes. Ripe
seeds blackish, triangu-
lar in end view, a little
smaller than the trian-
gular form of Dotted
Smartweed.

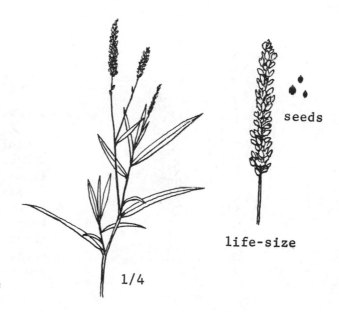

seeds

life-size

1/4

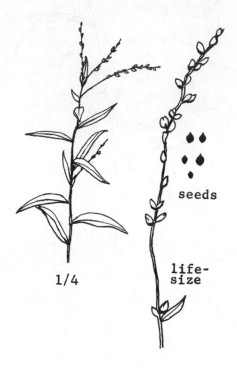

seeds

1/4   life-size

DOTTED SMARTWEED,
Polygonum punctatum
(Polygonum robustius, Persi-
caria punctata)

Inland and coastal fresh
marshes; British Columbia to
Quebec and the southernmost
States.
Stems less than knee-high
to as high as a man. Leaves
to 8 inches long. Flowers
whitish or greenish in loose,
usually straight spikes.
Flowers and leaves contain
oil which stings tongue and
lips. Ripe seeds brown to
black, either triangular or
biconvex in end view, the
triangular form a little
bigger than the seed of Swamp
Smartweed.

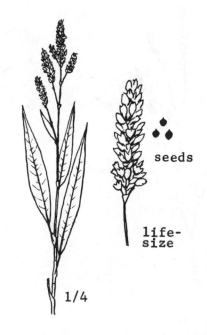

seeds

life-size

1/4

SOUTHERN SMARTWEED,
Polygonum densiflorum
(Persicaria portoricensis)

Inland and coastal fresh
marshes; Kansas to New Jersey,
Texas, and Florida.
Stems knee-high to as high
as a man. Leaves to one foot
long. Flowers white or pink
in straight spikes. Ripe
seeds blackish, biconvex in
end view.

HAIRY SMARTWEED,
Polygonum hirsutum
(Persicaria hirsuta)

Inland fresh marshes;
North Carolina to Florida.
    Stems knee-high to
waist-high, usually shaggy
with long hairs. Leaves
wide-based, to 4 inches
long. Flowers white or
pinkish, in straight
spikes. Ripe seeds black-
ish, triangular in end
view.

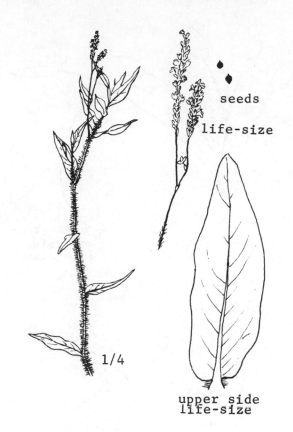

seeds

life-size

1/4

upper side
life-size

HALBERDLEAF TEAR-THUMB,
Polygonum arifolium
(Tracaulon arifolium)

Inland and coastal fresh
marshes; Minnesota to Prince
Edward Island, Texas, and
Florida.
    Stems to several feet
long, usually leaning on
other plants and clinging by
down-pointing prickles along
stems and along the midvein
on the underside of leaves.
Leaves to 8 inches long.
flowers pink, greenish, or
white, in little clusters.
Ripe seeds brown to black,
thick-biconvex in end view.

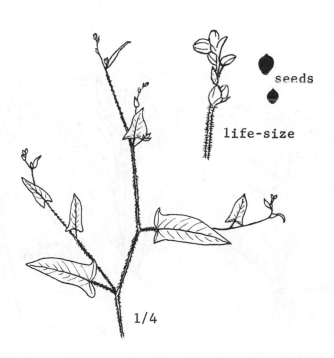

seeds

life-size

1/4

51

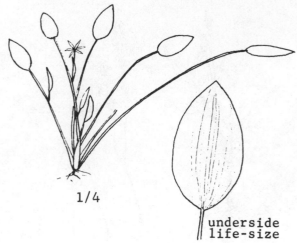

1/4

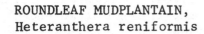

underside
life-size

LONGLEAF MUDPLANTAIN,
Heteranthera limosa

Inland fresh marshes and
water; California; Colorado to
Minnesota, Arizona, Louisiana,
and Kentucky.
   Stems sprawling and out of
water, or floating. Leaves
with about a dozen lengthwise-
running main veins, and with
finer veins between. Flowers
blue or white, singly placed.

ROUNDLEAF MUDPLANTAIN,
Heteranthera reniformis

Inland and coastal fresh
marshes and water; Kansas to
Connecticut, Texas, and
Florida.
   Stems sprawling and out of
water, or floating. Leaves
with 30 or 40 lengthwise-
running main veins, and with
finer veins between. Flowers
white or blue, 2 to 16 in a
cluster.

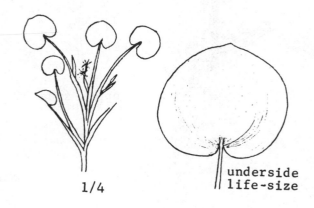

1/4

underside
life-size

FLOATING WATERPRIMROSE,
Jussiaea repens
(Jussiaea californica
and diffusa)

Inland fresh marshes;
California to Arizona;
Kansas to New Jersey,
Texas and Alabama.
   Stems sprawling to
partly floating, usually
upright toward tip, to
10 feet long. Leaves
oval or lance-shaped,
to 3 inches long.
Flowers yellow, usually
less than 1 inch across.

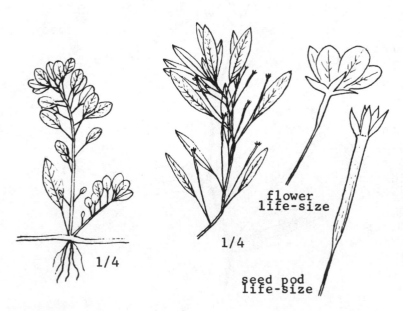

1/4

1/4

flower
life-size

seed pod
life-size

52

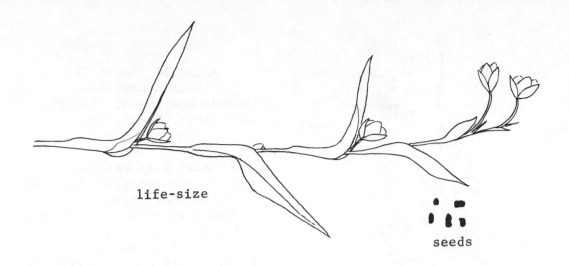

life-size

seeds

MARSH DAYFLOWER, Aneilema keisak

Coastal and inland fresh marshes; Virginia to Georgia.
Stems horizontal or leaning on other plants, 1 to 5 feet long.
Leaves to 2 1/2 inches long. Flowers pink, placed singly at
the base of leaves.   Seed pods oval when ripe, with a few dark-
gray, flattish, variable-sized seeds. In side view, some seeds
appear cut off at one end.

MARSH BOLTONIA,
Boltonia asteroides
(Boltonia latisquama)

Inland and coastal fresh
marshes; Oregon to Idaho;
Saskatchewan to Maine,
Texas, and Florida.
Stems less than knee-
high to as high as a man
branched toward the top.
Leaves to 6 inches long.
Flower heads white or
pinkish. Ripe seeds
light-brown, flat, with
two tiny bristles at
the top.

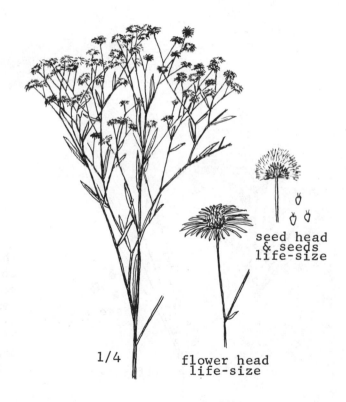

seed head
& seeds
life-size

1/4

flower head
life-size

seeds
life-size

life-size

ATLANTIC SEA-BLITE,
Suaeda maritima
(Suaeda americana, linearis,
and richii; Dondia linearis
and maritima)

Coastal salt marshes;
Alaska to Washington; Manitoba
to Quebec and Texas.
Stems sprawling to upright
and thigh-high, branched.
Leaves to 2 inches long,
fleshy, half-round to roundish
in cross section. Flowers
tiny, greenish, in small clusters at the base of many upper
leaves. Ripe seeds blackish,
biconvex in end view.

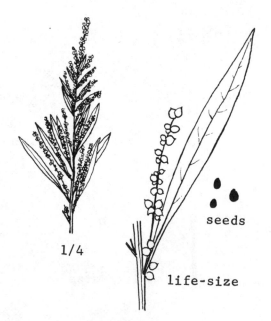

1/4

seeds

life-size

TIDEMARSH WATERHEMP,
Amaranthus cannabinus
(Acnida cannabina)

Coastal fresh and slightly
brackish marshes; Maine to
Florida.
Stems knee-high to higher
than a man, branched. Leaves
to 8 inches long. Flowers
small, greenish, the male and
female on separate plants.
Ripe seeds dark brown to
black, flattish in end view
and slightly concave on the
sides.

54

ANNUAL SALTMARSH ASTER,
    Aster subulatus

    Coastal salt to fresh
marshes; New Brunswick to
Louisiana. Rarely inland
salt marshes in Michigan
and New York.
    Stems ankle-high to
waist-high, branched,
coming from annual roots.
Leaves to 6 inches long.
Flower heads to 1/2 inch
across, their bluish
rays so short that they
barely show.

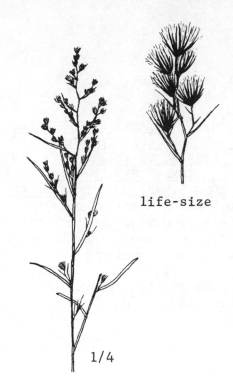

life-size

1/4

PERENNIAL SALTMARSH ASTER,
    Aster tenuifolius

    Coastal salt and brack-
ish marshes; New Hampshire
to Mississippi.
    Stems ankle-high to
knee-high, branched or
unbranched, coming from a
perennial rootstock.
Leaves to 6 inches long.
Flower heads to 3/4 inch
across, with bluish or
whitish rays.

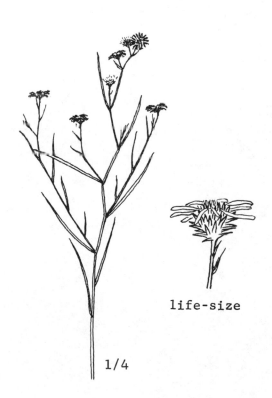

life-size

1/4

Group 5. <u>PLANTS WITH UPRIGHT, SPRAWLING, OR HORIZONTAL STEMS WITH</u>
<u>PAIRED, WHORLED, OR OTHERWISE CLUSTERED, LANCE-SHAPED OR WIDER, UN-</u>
<u>TOOTHED LEAVES; OR PLANTS WITH LEAFLESS STEMS AND PAIRED OR WHORLED</u>
<u>BRANCHES; FLOWERS SINGLE OR CLUSTERED AT THE END OF STEMS, IN STALKED</u>
<u>HEADS ALONG STEMS, OR SINGLE OR CLUSTERED AT THE BASE OF LEAVES</u>;
growing inland in fresh and alkali marshes and along the coasts in
fresh to salt marshes. Stems are close to each other in colonies, or
scattered. In some kinds they come up year after year from underground,
underwater, or creeping stems, in others each year from seed. They
vary from sometimes under water in Marestail to as high as a man in
Purple Loosestrife. Leaves of Sea-oxeye sometimes have little teeth
near the base. Flowers are white, greenish, yellow, blue, pink, or
reddish.

MARESTAIL,
Hippuris vulgaris
(Hippuris tetraphylla)

Inland fresh and coastal brackish marshes and water; Alaska to Greenland, California, New Mexico, Iowa, and New York.

Stems usually upright and ankle-high to less than waist-high; sometimes under water and limp. Leaves 1/4 to 1 1/2 inches long. Each tiny flower at the base of a leaf produces one seed. Ripe seeds are round in end view.

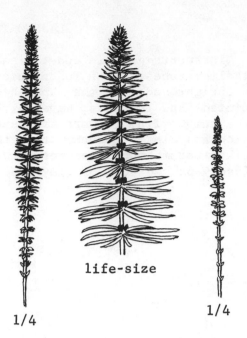

life-size

1/4   1/4

WATER HORSETAIL,
Equisetum fluviatile

Inland and occasionally coastal fresh marshes; Alaska to Newfoundland, Oregon, Nebraska, and West Virginia.

Stems knee-high to shoulder-high, conspicuously jointed, not evergreen, thin-walled around a big hollow center, usually with whorled branches, often with a spore-producing cone at the tip.

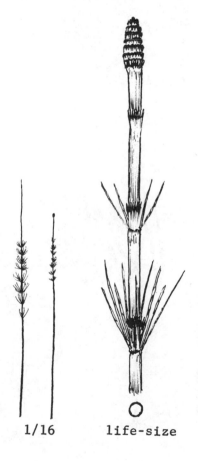

1/16   life-size

GLASSWORTS, Salicornia

Glassworts grow in coastal salt marshes and in inland salt and alkali marshes, often in colonies. Their stems are ground-carpeting to upright and less than knee-high. They are fleshy, conspicuously jointed, and leafless; have paired branches; and often are bright red in autumn. Tiny flowers are sunk in the upper part of stems, at joints which are closer together than the joints farther down. These flower spikes become more distinctive when their seeds have fallen, leaving closely packed rows of tiny cups.

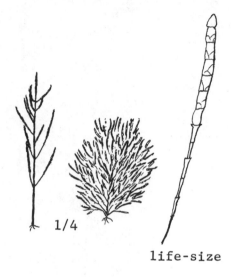

1/4

life-size

SLENDER GLASSWORT,
Salicornia europaea
(Salicornia depressa and rubra)

Coastal salt marshes and inland salt and alkali marshes; Alaska to Newfoundland, California, Texas, and Georgia (but rare inland in the eastern half of the continent).
Pulls up easily because of annual roots. Stems upright or sprawly. Spikes usually less than 3/16 inch in diameter, the sections between their joints as long as thick, or longer.

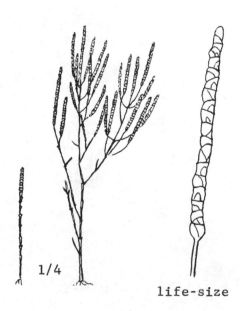

1/4

life-size

BIGELOW GLASSWORT,
Salicornia bigelovii

Coastal and very rarely inland salt marshes; California; New Mexico; Maine to Texas.
Resembles Slender Glasswort; but Bigelow Glasswort spikes are 3/16 to 1/4 inch in diameter, and the sections between their joints are shorter than thick.

WOODY GLASSWORT,
Salicornia virginica
(Salicornia pacifica
and perennis)

Coastal salt marshes and
rarely inland salt and
alkali marshes; Alaska to
California and New Mexico;
New Hampshire to Texas.
Has rootstocks and often
has horizontal main stems.
Spikes have nontapering
tips with flowers all the
way to the end.

1/4   life-size

CALIFORNIA GLASSWORT,
Salicornia subterminalis
(Arthrocnemum subterminale)

Coastal salt marshes
and inland alkali marshes;
California.
Resembles Woody Glass-
wort; but California Glasswort spikes have tapering
tips which are flowerless.

1/4   life-size

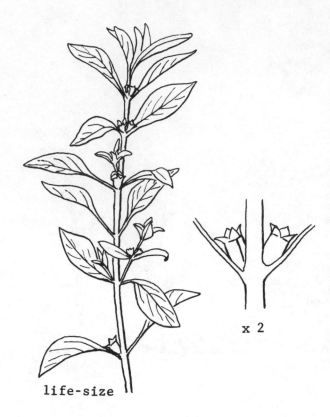

MARSH-PURSLANE,
Ludwigia palustris
(Ludwigia natans; Isnar-
dia intermedia, palustris,
and repens)

Inland and coastal
fresh marshes and water;
British Columbia to Nova
Scotia and the southern-
most States.
Stems usually sprawl-
ing on wet ground or
partly in water; some-
times under water in
springs and clear
streams. Leaves 1/2
inch to 2 inches long,
green to reddish.
Flowers greenish to
reddish.

x 2

life-size

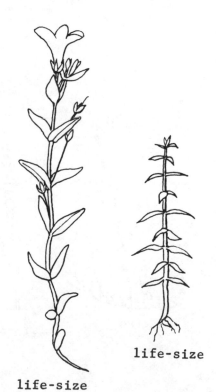

GOLDENPERT, Gratiola aurea

Inland fresh marshes and
water; Wisconsin to Newfoundland, Alabama, and Florida
(but only near the coast in
the South).
Out-of-water or partly-
out-of-water plants have
stems ankle-high to less
than knee-high, blunt-
tipped leaves, and yellow
flowers. Underwater plants
have stems an inch or two
high, sharp-tipped leaves,
and no flowers.

life-size

life-size

PURPLE LOOSESTRIFE,
Lythrum salicaria

Inland and coastal fresh
marshes; British Columbia
to Newfoundland, California,
Missouri, and North Caro-
lina (commonest in New
England and New York).
Stems waist-high to as
high as a man, fine-hairy.
Leaves in pairs or sometimes
in threes, to 4 inches long.
Flowers purplish-pink.

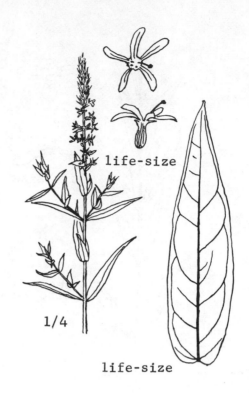

life-size

1/4

life-size

SWAMP LOOSESTRIFE,
Decodon verticillatus

Inland fresh marshes;
Minnesota to Nova Scotia,.
Louisiana, and Florida.
Stems curved and often
several feet long, their
tips reaching the ground or
water. Under water, the
bark is very thick and
spongy. Leaves in twos,
threes, or fours, to 6
inches long. Flowers
purplish-pink.

1/4

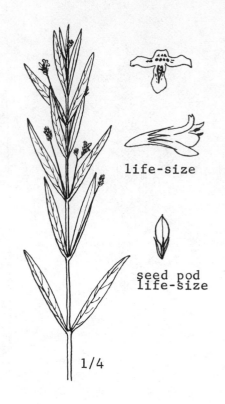

life-size

seed pod
life-size

1/4

WATERWILLOW,
Justicia americana
(Dianthera americana)

   Inland fresh marshes;
Kansas to Quebec, Texas,
and Georgia.
   Stems knee-high to
waist-high, in dense beds
in shallow water, more
often in streams than in
lakes. Leaves to 8
inches long. Flowers
whitish with purple spots,
in long-stalked heads.
Seed pods biconvex in end
view.

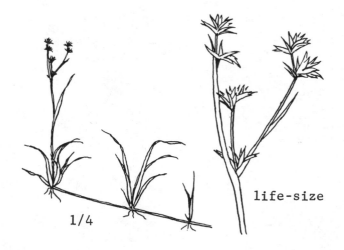

1/4

life-size

CREEPING RUSH,
Juncus repens

   Inland fresh
marshes and water,
Oklahoma to Dela-
ware, Texas, and
Florida.
   Sprawling on wet
ground, floating,
or under water.
Stems and leaves
flattish. Flowers
green.

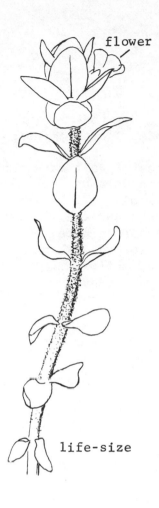

flower

life-size

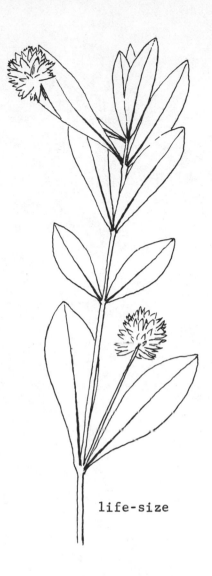

life-size

LEMON BACOPA,
Bacopa caroliniana
(Hydrotrida caroliniana)

Inland fresh marshes;
Virginia to Texas and
Florida.
Stems ankle-high to
knee-high, hairy toward
the top. Crushed leaves
and stems lemon-scented.
Flowers blue.

ALLIGATORWEED,
Alternanthera philoxeroides
(Achyranthes philoxeroides)

Inland and coastal fresh
marshes; Tennessee to Virginia, Texas, and Florida.
Stems sprawling to partly
floating, upright toward tip,
to several feet long. Leaves
to 4 inches long. Flowers
whitish.

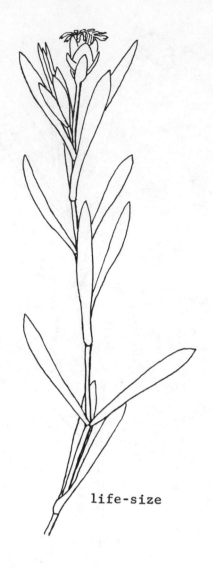

JAUMEA, Jaumea carnosa

    Coastal salt marshes;
British Columbia to
California.
    Stems ankle-high
to less than knee-
high, topped with a
head of yellow
flowers. Leaves
fleshy.

life-size

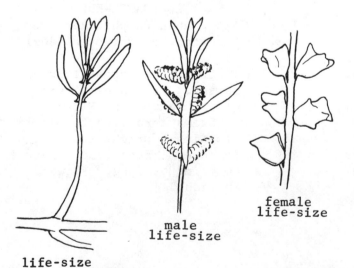

SALTWORT, Batis maritima

    Coastal salt marshes;
California; North Caro-
lina to Texas.
    Stems sprawling,
branched, ankle-high to
waist-high. Leaves
light-green, fleshy,
half-round in cross sec-
tion, with a tiny spur
at the base. Tiny male
and female flowers in
spikes on separate
plants.

life-size

male
life-size

female
life-size

SALTFLAT-GLASS,
Monanthochloe littoralis

    Coastal salt marshes;
California; Texas to
Florida.
    Main stems horizontal,
branches ankle-high to
less than knee-high.
Flowers almost hidden
among leaves.

life-size

FRANKENIA,
Frankenia grandifolia

    Coastal salt marshes
and inland alkali
marshes; California.
    Stems ankle-high to
less than knee-high,
much-branched, smooth
or fine-hairy. Leaves
paired or clustered,
their edges often
rolled under, making the
smaller, upper ones look
quite narrow. Flowers
pinkish.

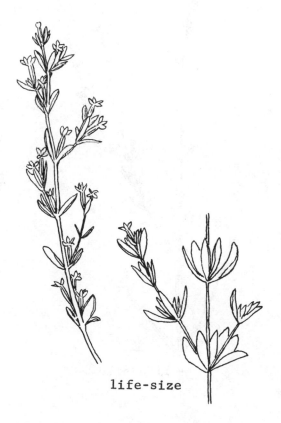

life-size

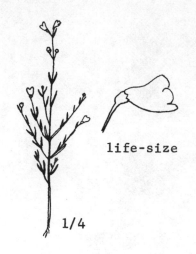

life-size

1/4

SEASIDE GERARDIA,
Gerardia maritima
(Agalinis maritima)

Coastal salt marshes; Nova
Scotia to Texas.
Stems ankle-high to knee-
high, branched or unbranched.
Leaves to an inch long.
Flowers purplish-pink, fine-
hairy inside and outside.

SALTMARSH LOOSESTRIFE,
Lythrum lineare

Coastal salt and brackish
marshes; New Jersey to Texas.
Stems less than knee-high
to waist-high, much-branched
toward the top, hairless.
Leaves to an inch long.
Flowers whitish or pinkish.

life-size

LITTLE SEA-PINK
Sabatia stellaris
(part of Sabatia campanu-
lata in Small's Manual)

Coastal salt and brack-
ish marshes; Massachusetts
to Louisiana. Inland
marshes in Florida.
Stems ankle-high to
knee-high, branched or unbranched. Leaves to
1 1/2 inches long.
Flowers pink with yellow
center, usually with 5
petals.

1/4   life-size

BIG SEA-PINK,
Sabatia dodecandra
(Sabatia foliosa and
harperi)

Coastal salt and brack-
ish marshes and inland
fresh marshes; Connecticut
to Louisiana.
Stems ankle-high to less
than waist-high, branched.
Leaves to 2 inches long.
Flowers pink with yellow
center, with 8 to 12
petals.

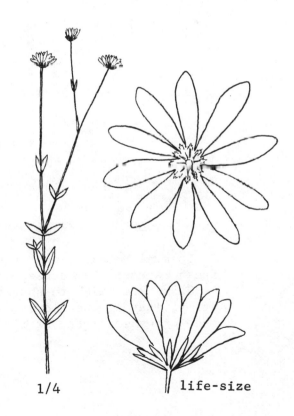

1/4   life-size

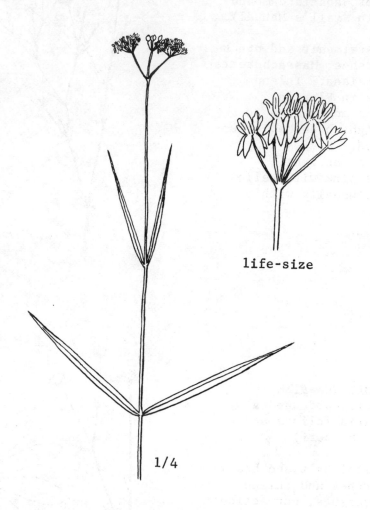

life-size

1/4

COAST MILKWEED, Asclepias lanceolata

    Coastal brackish and fresh marshes and rarely inland
fresh marshes; New Jersey to Texas.
    Stems knee-high to shoulder-high, not branched.
Stems, leaves, and flower clusters all slender. Petals
red, crown in center of flower orange.

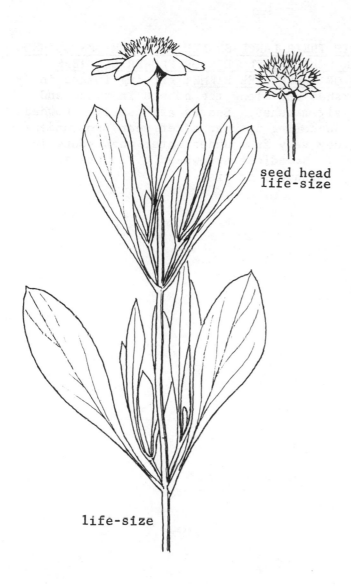

seed head
life-size

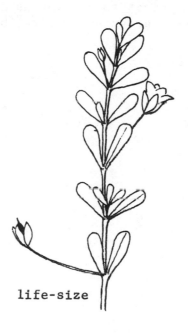

life-size

life-size

COAST BACOPA,
Bacopa monnieri
(Bramia monnieri)

Coastal brackish and
fresh marshes; Virginia
to Texas. Inland
marshes in Texas.
Stems carpeting the
ground to ankle-high,
hairless. Leaves fleshy.
Flowers whitish.

SEA-OXEYE, Borrichia frutescens

Coastal salt marshes; Virginia
to Texas.
Stems ankle-high to waist-high,
woody, branched, topped with a
head of yellow flowers. Leaves
grayish, 1 to 4 inches long, their
edges untoothed or with little
teeth near the base. Seed head
burlike because of sharp, hard
bracts.

Group 6. <u>PLANTS WITH BOTH THEIR LANCE-SHAPED OR WIDER, UNTOOTHED</u> <u>LEAVES AND THE STALKS OF THEIR SOLITARY FLOWERS OR FLOWER CLUSTERS</u> <u>COMING FROM UNDERGROUND STEMS OR UNDERWATER STEMS</u>; growing inland in fresh and rarely in alkali marshes and along the coasts in fresh and occasionally in brackish and salt marshes. Leaves are usually crowded in clusters, those of most kinds coming up year after year from underground or underwater stems. They vary from under water when young in some kinds to as high as a man in Broadleaf Arrowhead. Flowers are white, greenish, yellow, blue, lavender, or pink.

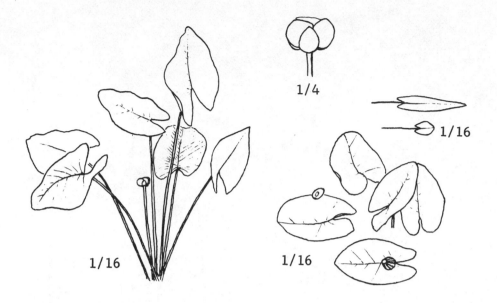

SPATTERDOCK, Nuphar luteum
(All Nuphar in Fernald's Manual, Nuphar polysepalum in Mason's Flora,
and all Nymphaea in Small's Manual)

Inland and coastal fresh marshes and water; Alaska to Newfoundland and the southernmost States.
    Leaves vary greatly in size and shape. In Canada, western
United States, and the northeastern States they usually float; in
the rest of eastern United States they often stand above water.
Flowers greenish outside and yellow or reddish inside, 3/4 inch to
3 inches across. Seed pods ball-shaped, with sides pinched in just
below the flattish top, 1/2 inch to 2 inches through. Ripe seeds
brown, oval, 1/8 to 1/4 inch long.

AMERICAN LOTUS,
   Nelumbo lutea

    Inland and rarely
coastal fresh marshes
and water; Minnesota
to Massachusetts,
Texas, and Florida.
    Leaves grayish-
green, to 2 feet
across, standing above
water or floating.
Flowers pale-yellow,
to 10 inches across,
fragrant. Ripe seeds
acornlike, partly ex-
posed in a flat-topped
pod.

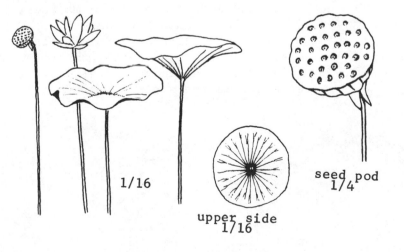

71

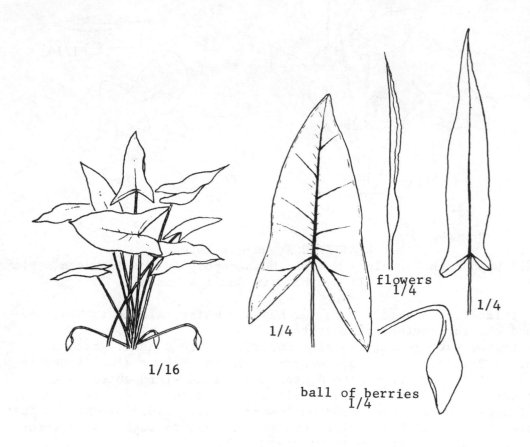

1/16

1/4

flowers
1/4

1/4

ball of berries
1/4

ARROW-ARUM, Peltandra virginica

Inland and coastal fresh marshes; Michigan to
Quebec, Texas, and Florida.
Leaves to waist-high, their blades varying
greatly in size and shape. Tiny flowers in a
green sheath produce an oval ball of berries
on a downcurved stalk.

PICKERELWEED,
Pontederia cordata
(Pontederia lanceolata)

Inland and coastal
fresh marshes; Minnesota
to Nova Scotia, Texas,
and Florida.
Leaves knee-high to
waist-high, their blades
varying from very narrow
to wider than shown in
the drawing. Flower
stalks with one leaf
below a spike of violet-
blue flowers.

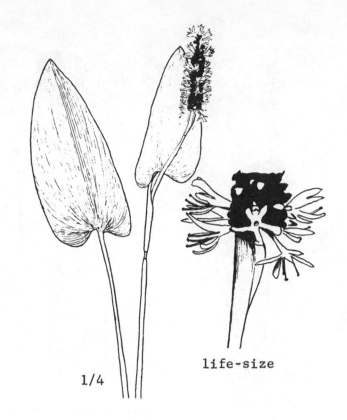

life-size

1/4

ARROWHEADS, Sagittaria

Arrowheads grow in fresh marshes and water, inland and along both
coasts, and in brackish marshes on the Atlantic Coast. Their clumps
of long-stalked leaves and long-stalked clusters of flowers are ankle-
high to higher than a man. The leaves vary greatly in size and shape.
Mature leaves of Northern, Broadleaf, Engelmann, Hooded, and Long-barb
Arrowheads are usually arrowhead-shaped. Those of Bur Arrowhead,
Slender Arrowhead, Delta Duckpotato, and Bulltongue are linear to oval,
and usually have no basal lobes. Young plants of some kinds grow under
water as clumps of stalkless leaves which vary from short and stiff to
long and ribbonlike. One kind, not described here, often grows to
maturity at the surface of the water or just under it. Arrowheads have
3-petaled white flowers which are usually whorled in threes. Flowers
of the lower whorls produce balls of tightly packed, flattish seeds.
Without ripe seeds it is hard to identify most kinds. All but Hooded
Arrowhead produce overwintering corms at the end of rootstocks. These
are eaten by waterfowl and muskrats, and occasionally by people.

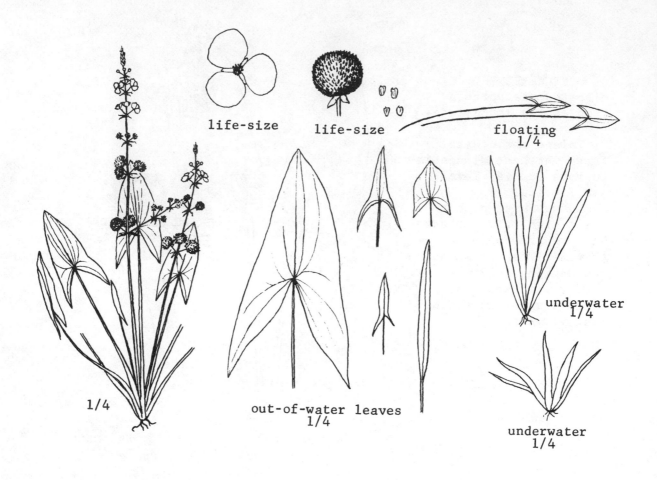

life-size   life-size   floating
1/4

1/4   out-of-water leaves   underwater
1/4   1/4

underwater
1/4

NORTHERN ARROWHEAD, Sagittaria cuneata

Inland and rarely coastal fresh marshes; Alaska to Quebec, California, Texas, and Pennsylvania.

Leaves varying greatly in size and shape, those of mature plants usually arrowhead-shaped. Leaves and flower clusters ankle-high to knee-high. Ripe seed balls look fine-prickly, because the seeds have a tiny upright point on one side of the top.

Resembles Broadleaf Arrowhead, but the ripe seed balls of that species look streaked and its seeds have a horizontal point at the top. Resembles Engelmann Arrowhead, but the ripe seed balls of that species look fine-bristly and its seeds have a prominent upright or upcurved point on one side of the top.

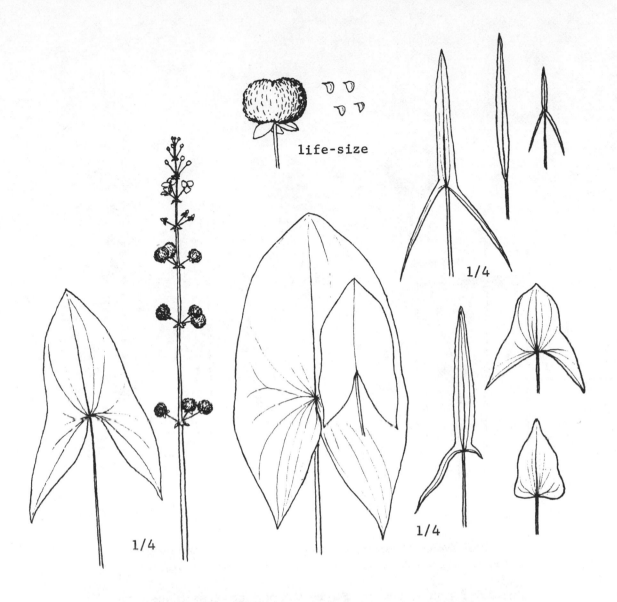

life-size

1/4

1/4

1/4

1/4

BROADLEAF ARROWHEAD, Sagittaria latifolia
(Sagittaria ornithorhyncha, planipes, and pubescens)

Inland and rarely coastal fresh marshes; British Columbia
to Quebec and the southernmost States (but very rare in the
Rocky Mountain region).

Flower clusters and variable leaves resemble those of
Northern Arrowhead, except that the leaves are sometimes as
high as a man, with blades to 20 inches long. Ripe seed balls
look streaked, because the seeds have a horizontal point at the
top.

Resembles Northern Arrowhead, but the ripe seed balls of
that species look fine-prickly and its seeds have a tiny
upright point on one side of the top. Resembles Engelmann
Arrowhead, but the ripe seed balls of that species look
fine-bristly and its seeds have an upright or upcurved
point on one side of the top.

75

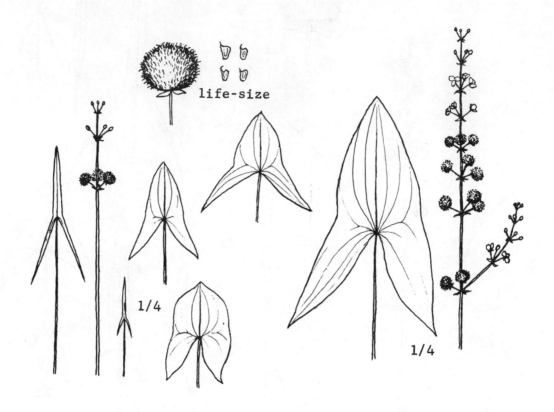

life-size

1/4

1/4

ENGELMANN ARROWHEAD, Sagittaria engelmanniana)
(Sagittaria australis, brevirostra, and longirostra)

Inland fresh marshes; South Dakota to Massachusetts,
Texas, and Florida.

Flower clusters and variable leaves resemble those of
Northern Arrowhead, except that the leaves are often
waist-high, with blades to 15 inches long. Ripe seed
balls look fine-bristly, because the seeds have an upright
or upcurved point on one side of the top.

Resembles Northern Arrowhead, but the ripe seed balls
of that species look fine-prickly and its seeds have a
tiny upright point on one side of the top. Resembles
Broadleaf Arrowhead, but the ripe seed balls of that
species look streaked and its seeds have a horizontal
point at the top.

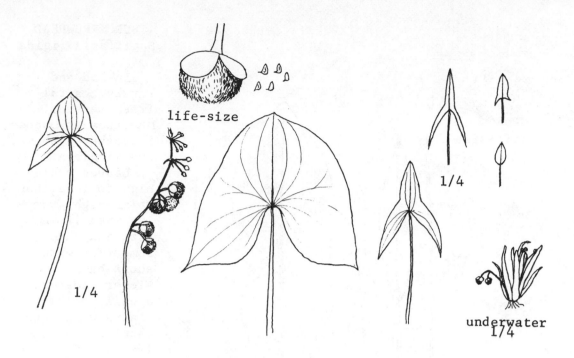

life-size

1/4

1/4

1/4

underwater
1/4

HOODED ARROWHEAD, Sagittaria calycina
(Lophotocarpus calycinus and spongiosus)

Inland and east-coast fresh marshes; California; South Dakota to
New Brunswick, New Mexico, Louisiana, and North Carolina.
Leaves ankle-high to knee-high, varying greatly in size and shape;
those of mature inland plants usually arrowhead-shaped and often
wider than long. Flower clusters often shorter than leaves. Ripe
seed balls partly covered by enlarged sepals, and on a downcurved
stalk. Seeds with a horizontal or upslanted point on one side of
the top.

LONG-BARB ARROWHEAD,
Sagittaria longiloba
(Sagittaria greggii)

Inland fresh marshes;
California to Nebraska
and Texas.
Flower clusters less
than knee-high to shoulder-
high, often higher than
leaves. Basal lobes of
leaves about twice as
long as upper lobe.
Ripe seed balls look
warty. Ripe seeds
with a tiny horizontal
or upslanted point on
one side of the top.

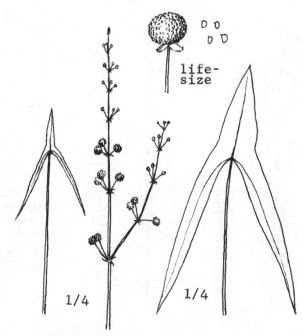

life-
size

1/4

1/4

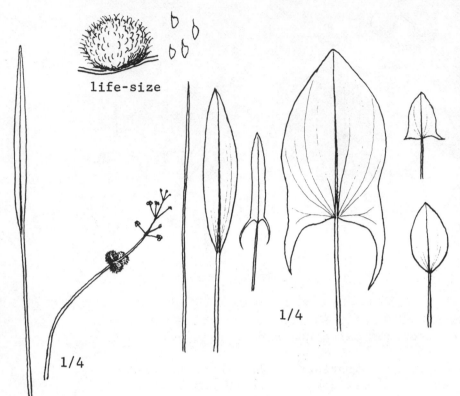

BUR ARROWHEAD, Sagittaria rigida

Inland and rarely coastal fresh marshes; Manitoba to Quebec, Nebraska, Alabama, and Virginia.

Leaves ankle-high to less than waist-high, varying greatly in size and shape, sometimes with short basal lobes. Flower clusters usually on bent stalks which are shorter than the leaves. Ripe seed balls short-stalked or stalkless. They look bristly, because the seeds have a prominent upright or upcurved point on one side of the top.

life-size

1/4

1/4

1/4

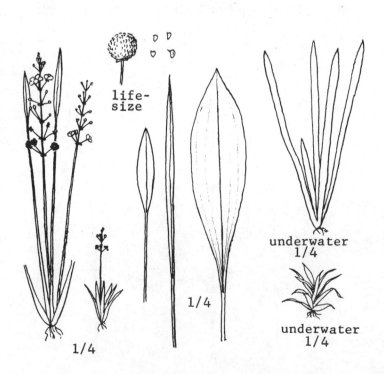

SLENDER ARROWHEAD, Sagittaria graminea (Sagittaria chapmanii, cristata, cycloptera, eatoni, isoetiformis, macrocarpa, teres, and weatherbiana)

Inland and occasionally coastal fresh marshes; South Dakota to Labrador, Texas, and Florida.

Flower clusters and linear to oval leaves ankle-high to less than waist-high. Ripe seed balls look warty. Ripe seeds with a tiny horizontal or upslanted point on one side of the top.

life-size

1/4

1/4

underwater
1/4

underwater
1/4

DELTA DUCKPOTATO,
Sagittaria platyphylla
(Sagittaria mohrii)

Inland and coastal
fresh marshes; Kansas
to North Carolina,
Texas, and Alabama.
Leaves less than
knee-high to waist-
high. Flower clus-
ters usually shorter
than leaves. Ripe
seed balls on a
downcurved stalk.
They look fine-
prickly, because
seeds have a
tiny upslanted point
on one side of the top.

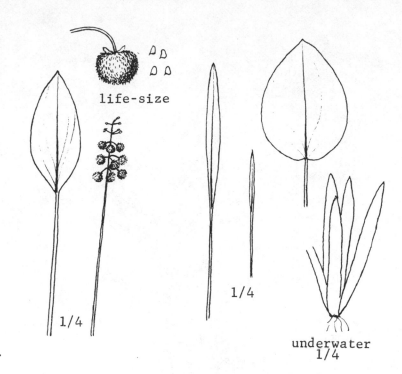

BULLTONGUE,
Sagittaria lancifolia
(Sagittaria angustifo-
lia and falcata)

Coastal fresh and
slightly brackish
marshes; Delaware to
Florida and Texas.
Inland fresh marshes
in Florida.
Flower clusters
knee-high to higher
than a man, often
higher than leaves.
Leaf blades in inland
Florida to 2 feet
long. Ripe seed balls
look fine-prickly,
because the seeds have
a tiny upslanted point
on one side of the top.

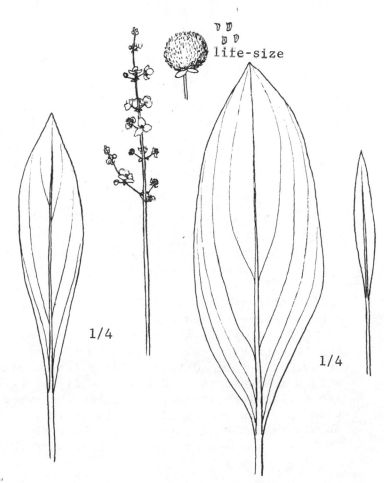

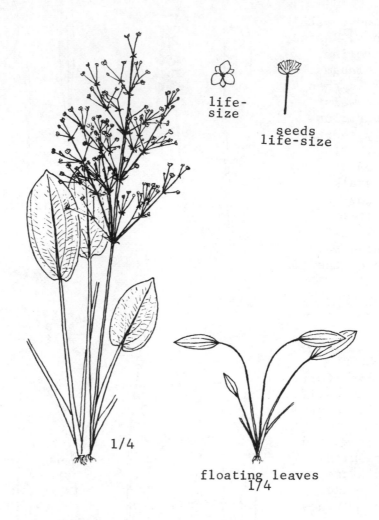

life-
size

seeds
life-size

1/4

floating leaves
1/4

BROADLEAF WATERPLANTAIN, Alisma plantago-aquatica
(Alisma subcordatum and triviale)

Inland fresh marshes; British Columbia to Nova Scotia and
the southernmost States.
Flower clusters ankle-high to waist-high, usually higher than
the leaves which have a blade to 10 inches long with a roundish
or slightly notched base. Early leaves often floating and
with a somewhat tapered base. White or rarely pink flowers
1/4 to 1/2 inch across, 3-petaled. Flowers throughout a
cluster produce a little circle of seeds which, as seen from
above, resembles a cut orange. Ripe seeds are less than 1/8
inch long and are grooved on their outer edges.

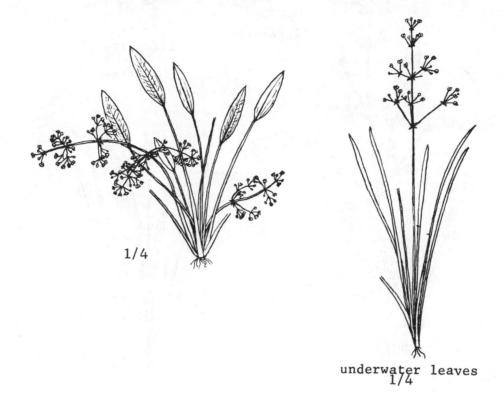

1/4

underwater leaves
1/4

NARROWLEAF WATERPLANTAIN, Alisma gramineum
(Alisma geyeri)

   Inland fresh and alkali marshes and water; Alberta to
Quebec, California, Iowa, and Vermont.
   Flower clusters sprawling to knee-high, shorter or longer
than leaves. Out-of-water leaves have a blade to 4 inches
long, with a somewhat tapered base. Underwater leaves are
usually ribbonlike and as much as 3 feet long. Ripe seeds
and the white or pink flowers are similar to those of
Broadleaf Waterplantain.

81

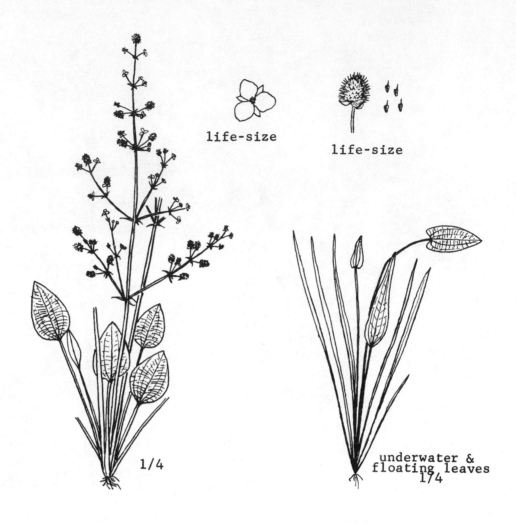

life-size

life-size

1/4

underwater &
floating leaves
1/4

UPRIGHT BURHEAD, Echinodorus berteroi
(Echinodorus cordifolius in Mason's Flora and Small's Manual,
Echinodorus rostratus in Fernald's Manual)

Inland fresh marshes; California to Arizona; South Dakota to
Ohio, Texas, and Florida.
Flower clusters ankle-high to knee-high, usually higher than
the leaves which have blades to 8 inches long. Early leaves
often floating or under water. White flowers about 1/2 inch
across, 3-petaled. Flowers throughout a cluster produce a
ball of tightly packed seeds which, when ripe, look fine-bristly, because the seeds have a prominent upright point at the top.
Resembles Creeping Burhead; but full-grown flower clusters of
that species are usually horizontal, its ripe seed balls look
fine-prickly, and its seeds have a tiny upslanted point on one
side of the top.

82

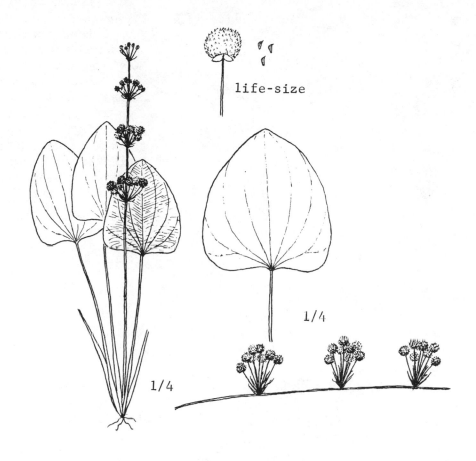

life-size

1/4

1/4

CREEPING BURHEAD, Echinodorus cordifolius
(Echinodorus radicans; not Echinodorus cordifolius of
Mason's Flora and Small's Manual)

Inland fresh marshes; Kansas to D. C., Texas, and Florida.
Flower clusters usually horizontal or sprawling, to 4 feet
long. Leaf blades to 8 inches long. Flowers similar to
Upright Burhead except a little larger. Ripe seed balls look
fine-prickly, because the seeds have a tiny upslanted point on
one side of the top.
Resembles Upright Burhead; but full-grown flower clusters of
that species are upright, its ripe seed balls look fine-bristly,
and its seeds have a prominent upright point at the top.

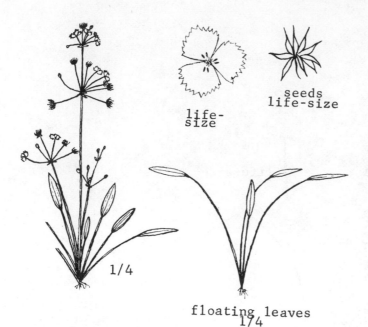

life-
size

seeds
life-size

DAMASONIUM,
Damasonium californicum

Inland fresh marshes
and water; Oregon to
California and Nevada.
Flower clusters to
less than knee-high, or
sprawling. Leaf blades
to 3 inches long.
Early leaves often
floating. Flowers
white or pink with
yellow center.

1/4

floating leaves
1/4

SEA-LAVENDER
Limonium vulgare
(Limonium angustatum, caro-
linianum, commune, nashii,
and obtusilobum)

Coastal salt marshes
and rarely inland alkali
marshes; California; New
Mexico; Newfoundland to
Texas.
Flower clusters ankle-
high to knee-high, two or
three times as high as the
leathery leaves. Flowers
lavender, 5-petaled, close
to each other along the
branches.

1/4

GOLDENCLUB,
Orontium aquaticum

Inland and coastal
fresh marshes and
water; Kentucky to
Massachusetts, Louis-
iana, and Florida.
Leaves to knee-
high, or floating,
their upper side with
a satiny sheen. Tiny
flowers are in a
yellow spike on an
upwardly thickened
white stalk.

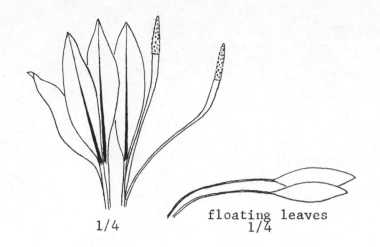

1/4

floating leaves
1/4

AMERICAN FROGBIT,
Limnobium spongia

Inland fresh marshes
and water; Missouri to
Delaware, Texas, and
Florida.
There are two forms.
One has rather leathery
out-of-water leaves;
the other has floating
leaves which are thick
and spongy in the center
and are deeply notched
at the base. Whitish,
narrow-petaled female
flowers grow on indi-
vidual stalks at the
base of a plant. They
produce a roundish seed
pod on a usually
downcurved stalk.

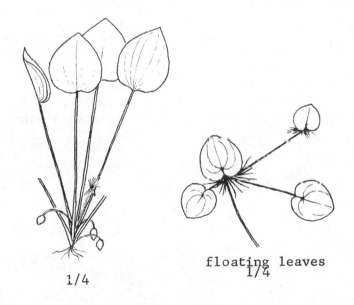

1/4

floating leaves
1/4

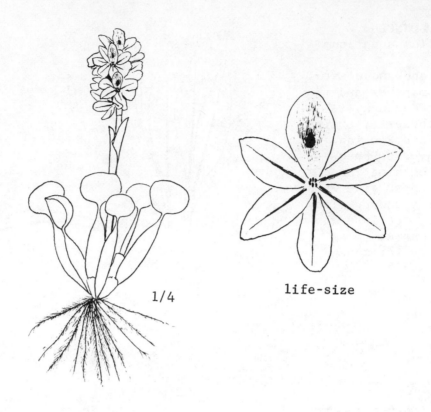

1/4

life-size

WATER-HYACINTH, Eichornia crassipes
(Piaropus crassipes)

Inland and coastal fresh marshes and water; California;
Missouri to Virginia, Texas, and Florida.
Usually floating, often in big, dense colonies, with leaves
and flowers reaching above the water. Leaf blades 2 to 4
inches across on a much-swollen stalk. Flowers lavender,
with an orange-centered bluish blotch on the uppermost petal.

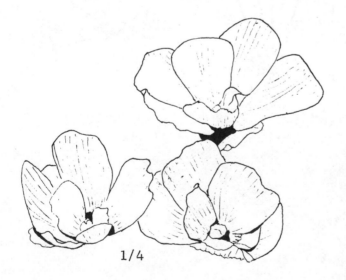

WATERLETTUCE,
Pistia stratiotes

Inland fresh marshes
and water; California to
Florida.
Usually floating, often
in dense colonies, with
grayish-green, conspic-
uously veined leaves
reaching above the water.
Leaves to 9 inches long.
Inconspicuous flowers
are at bases of leaves.

1/4

86

Group 7. <u>PLANTS WITH TOOTH-EDGED TO DEEPLY DIVIDED LEAVES OR LEAFLETS</u>; growing inland in fresh and rarely in alkali marshes and along the coasts in fresh to salt marshes. Stems are close to each other in groups, or scattered. In some kinds they come up year after year from underground, underwater, or creeping stems, in others each year from seed. They vary from sometime under water in Marsh Mermaidweed to higher than a man in Marsh Hibiscus. Flowers are white, greenish, yellow, pink, or purplish.

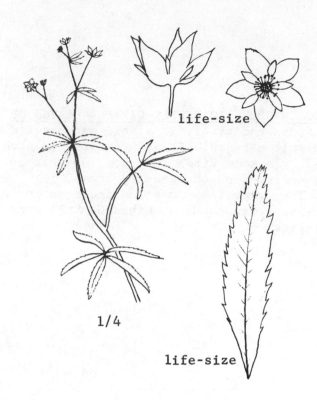

life-size

1/4

life-size

MARSH CINQUEFOIL,
Potentilla palustris

Inland fresh marshes;
Alaska to Greenland,
California, Wyoming, and
New Jersey.
Stems horizontal at
base, ankle-high to knee-
high at top. Leaflets
green or gray above,
gray beneath. Flowers
purplish-red, sepals
twice as long as petals.

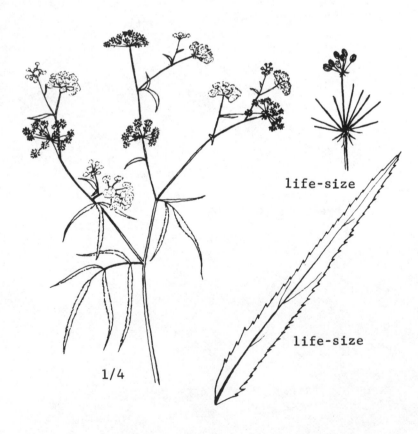

life-size

1/4

life-size

WATERPARSNIP,
Sium suave
(Sium cicutaefolium
and floridanum)

Inland and coast-
al fresh marshes;
Alaska to Newfound-
land and the south-
ernmost States.
Stems knee-high
to as high as a man.
Leaves compound,
their leaflets to
6 inches long.
Flowers white and
tiny, in compound
umbels.

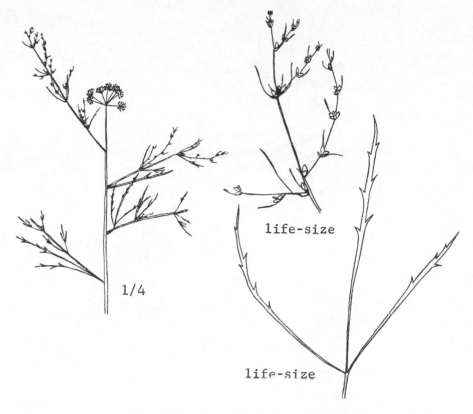

1/4

life-size

life-size

BULBLET WATERHEMLOCK, Cicuta bulbifera

Inland fresh marshes; Northwest Territories to Newfoundland, Oregon, Nebraska, and Virginia.
Stems knee-high to shoulder-high. Leaves compound, their leaflets to 2 1/2 inches long. Flowers white and tiny, in compound umbels; or sometimes no flowers. Bulblets common along upper branches. Roots very poisonous when eaten by domestic animals or people.

NODDING BEGGARTICKS, Bidens cernua
    (Bidens laevis and nashii)

Inland fresh marshes and coastal fresh and brackish marshes; Alaska to Quebec and the southernmost States.
Stems ankle-high to as high as a man. Leaves to 8 inches long. Flower heads yellow. Sometimes they are only a closely packed circle of tiny flowers; more often these tiny flowers are surrounded by as many as 10 rays which are as much as 1 1/2 inches long. Ripe seeds have barbed points which make the seeds stick to clothing.

seeds
life-size

1/4

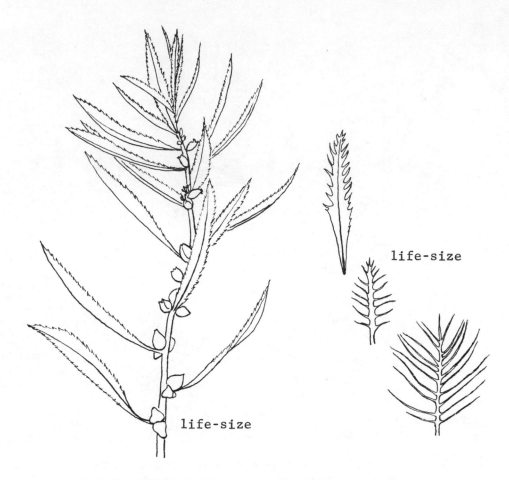

life-size

life-size

MARSH MERMAIDWEED, Proserpinaca palustris
(Proserpinaca amblyogona and platycarpa)

Inland and coastal fresh marshes; Wisconsin to Nova Scotia, Texas, and Florida.

Stems horizontal at base, ankle-high to knee-high at top. In winter, stems are under water and have featherlike leaves. In the growing season, the leaves vary from featherlike under water to tooth-edged and to 4 inches long on the out-of-water parts of stems. Each tiny greenish flower at the base of a leaf produces one seed. Ripe seeds are triangular in end view.

CUTLEAF MERMAIDWEED, Proserpinaca pectinata

Inland fresh marshes; Tennessee to Nova Scotia, Texas, and Florida.

Stems horizontal at base, ankle-high to less than knee-high at top. Leaves all featherlike, whether under water or out of water. Seeds similar to Marsh Mermaidweed.

life-size

PARROTFEATHER,
Myriophyllum brasiliense
(Myriophyllum proserpinacoides)

A common aquarium plant,
originally from South America,
which has become established
in inland fresh marshes and
water; Idaho to California
and Arizona; Kansas to New
York, Texas, and Florida.

Leaves firm and grayish-
green on the short part of
stems above water; limp
and with longer, narrower
leaflets on the part of
stems under water.

underwater
life-size

life-size

WATER-PARSLEY,
Oenanthe sarmentosa

Inland fresh marshes;
Alaska to California.

Stems sprawling, 2 to 5
feet long. Leaves compound,
their leaflets to 2 1/2
inches long. Flowers white
and tiny, in compound umbels.

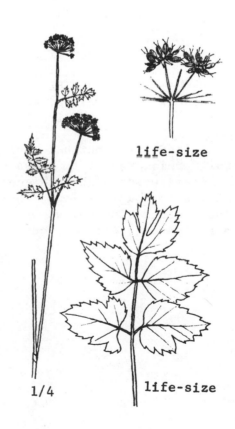

life-size

1/4

life-size

91

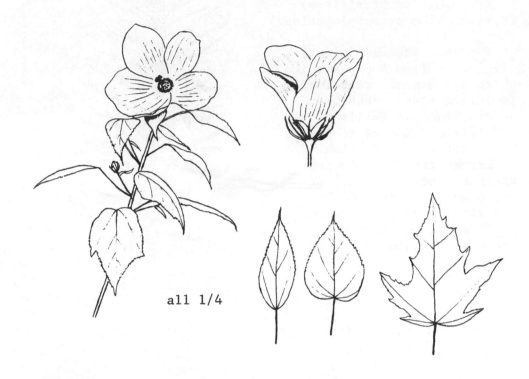

all 1/4

MARSH HIBISCUS, Hibiscus moscheutos
(Hibiscus californicus, grandiflorus, incanus, lasiocarpos,
oculiroseus, and palustris)

    Inland fresh marshes and coastal fresh and brackish marshes;
California; Kansas to Massachusetts, Texas, and Florida.
    Stems waist-high to higher than a man, usually in clumps.
Leaves to 8 inches long, their upper side hairless or hairy,
their under side hairy. Flowers white or pink, with or without
a red center, 4 to 8 inches across. Seed pods hairless or hairy.

SALTMARSH PLUCHEA,
Pluchea purpurascens
(Pluchea camphorata in Mason's Flora and Small's Manual)

Coastal brackish and inland alkali marshes; California to Kansas and Texas; Massachusetts to Texas.

Stems less than knee-high to waist-high. Leaves to 5 inches long. Flowers pink or purplish.

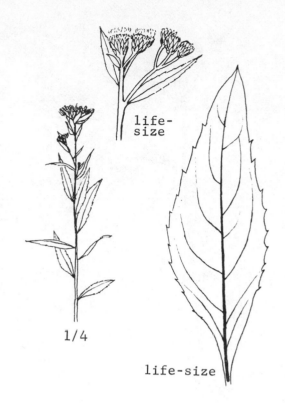

life-size

1/4

life-size

MOCK-BISHOPWEED,
Ptilimnium capillaceum

Coastal brackish and fresh marshes and inland fresh marshes; Missouri to Massachusetts, Texas, and Florida.

Stems ankle-high to less than waist-high. Leaves compound, their thread-thin leaflets to one inch long. Flowers white and tiny, in compound umbels.

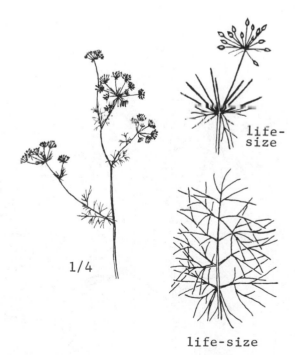

life-size

1/4

life-size

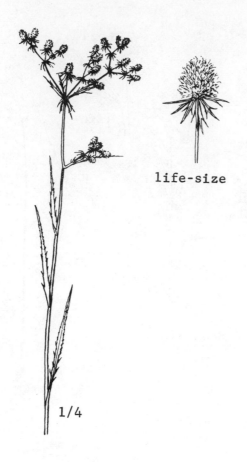

life-size

1/4

MARSH ERYNGO,
Eryngium aquaticum
(Eryngium floridanum, rave-
nelii, and virginianum)

Coastal fresh and brackish
marshes and occasionally inland fresh marshes; New
Jersey to Texas and Florida.
Stems knee-high to
shoulder-high. Lower leaves
long-stalked and with blades
to a foot long, their edges
often only slightly toothed.
Flowers whitish and tiny,
packed in bristly balls.

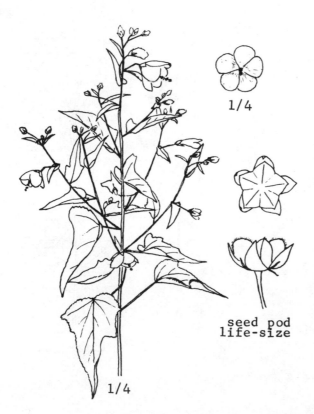

1/4

1/4

seed pod
life-size

1/4

SALTMARSH MALLOW,
Kosteletzkya virginica
(Kosteletzkya althaeifolia)

Coastal salt and brackish
marshes; New York to Florida
and Texas.
Stems knee-high to
shoulder-high. Leaves to
6 inches long. Flowers pink,
1 1/2 to 3 inches across.

I N D E X

Underwater and Floating-leaved Plants of the United States and Canada

CONTENTS

Page

UNDERWATER AND FLOATING-LEAVED PLANTS
OF THE UNITED STATES AND CANADA

This is the third of a series of circulars on field identification of North American marsh and water plants. It describes all of the wild flowering plants, ferns, liverworts, and Characeae in which the foliage is habitually under water or floating, and all those which have under-water or floating-leaved forms, and which, at the same time, have characteristics by which a person can tell them apart with the naked eye. If the different kinds cannot be told apart without a hand lens or microscope or when they are without flowers or seeds, only group descriptions are given.

To use this guide, a person should read pages 1 to 5 and the intro-ductions to each of the twelve groups, and should scan the pictures. Then, to identify a particular plant, he should find the group and the picture which match it, and read the description which goes with that picture. If the picture and description fit the plant, a name has been found for it.

These plants range from pinhead-size to twenty feet long. Most of the pictures are life-size or half life-size, as indicated; but many show no more than a sprig of a much-branched plant. This tells little of how an entire plant looks, or how dense patches look. But a person usually sees water plants from above them, then breaks off a piece for a closer look; or he salvages an already broken piece. So what is pictured here should be enough for identification.

Each description is headed with a common name and a scientific name. Under some of these headings, in parentheses, are one or more other scientific names which are used for the same plant in three commonly used manuals: Merritt Lyndon Fernald's "Gray's Manual of Botany, Eighth Edition" (1950); Herbert L. Mason's "A Flora of the Marshes of California" (1957); and John Kunkel Small's "Manual of the Southeastern Flora" (1933).

Seeds and rootstocks of many Pondweeds and of Widgeongrass, Wild-celery, Eelgrass, and Shoalgrass are important duck foods from fall to spring; and ducks, geese, muskrats, turtles, fish, insects, and other animals make some use of every plant described. When water plants get in the way of boating, swimming, or fishing they are quickly labeled "weeds". Then it's worth remembering that they protect bottoms from currents which stir up mud and sand, protect shores from waves, give fish places where temperatures are moderate and there is plenty of food and oxygen, and are interesting and beautiful.

1

Underwater plants are abundant in shallow, clear, still or slow-flowing, fresh water from southern British Columbia to southern Quebec, and south to the Great Basin, the Nebraska Sandhills, and the Great Lakes States. They are less common, but still in great variety, northwest to Alaska, northeast to Newfoundland, and east through New England. Farther north, short summers eliminate most of them. South of the main area they are only locally common because the water in most places is muddier, warmer, or more fluctuating than they can bear.

A few kinds (Eelgrass, Surfgrass, Shoalgrass, Manateegrass, Turtlegrass, and Halophilas) grow only in salt water in coastal bays, rivers, and creeks. Ribbonlike or threadlike green leaves distinguish them from the algae which grow nearby. Widgeongrass, Sago Pondweed, Horned-pondweed, Redhead-grass, and Eurasian Watermilfoil grow both inland and in fresh to brackish coastal water; and a larger number of mainly inland plants reach the coast in fresh to slightly brackish water.

Floating-leaved plants are occasional in fresh to slightly brackish water nearly everywhere that underwater plants are abundant or common. They are also common south along the Atlantic and Gulf Coastal Plain.

About half of the kinds of plants described here have flexible underwater stems which grow vertically, slantwise, or horizontally, and are thinly to densely covered with leaves or branchlets (Groups 3 to 8). The stems and foliage of most of these plants are so limp that when taken out of water for a closer look they slump into a characterless mass. To separate leaves and leaflets, a person can lay the plant flat and splash water over it; put it in a shallow dish of water; or shake the leaves apart after they have half-dried.

About one-fourth of the plants described grow under water, but have short stems or limp to stiff leaves coming up from the bottom (Groups 1 and 2).

Another fourth have leaves which float at the ends of stalks which come from the bottom or from flexible underwater stems, or leaves which float free of any attachment (Groups 9 to 12).

Many of the plants do not grow exclusively under water or on its surface. Some are under water as seedlings, and later produce floating leaves or out-of-water leaves. In others, the spring growth from over-wintering underground parts is under water; the mature growth reaches the surface of the water or above it. Some kinds have underwater, floating-leaved, and out-of-water forms which look so different that it is hard to believe they are related.

Floods temporarily submerged many kinds of plants that habitually live out of water and that cannot survive long under it. These are omitted.

The plants are discussed in twelve groups, each group beginning with northern inland plants and continuing through southern inland to strictly coastal ones.

Group 1.   Plants with limp, threadlike to ribbonlike leaves coming up from the bottom or from short vertical stems; sometimes partly floating (pages 5-13)

Slender Spikerush (see Group 2)	Wildcelery
Burreeds	Flowering-rush
Quillworts (see Group 2)	Eelgrass
Arrowheads (see Groups 2 & 10)	Surfgrass
Northern Mannagrass & Wildrice	Shoalgrass
Water Bulrush	Manateegrass
Narrowleaf Waterplantain	Turtlegrass

Group 2.   Plants with rather stiff, short leaves or nearly leafless stems in clumps or patches on the bottom; some kinds sometimes out of water (pages 14-30)

Slender Spikerush	Bog Rush
Creeping Buttercup	Horned Bladderwort
Quillworts	Zigzag Bladderwort
Subularia	Lavender Bladderwort
Arrowheads	Flowering-quillwort
Limosella	Pillwort
Water Lobelia	Western Lilaeopsis
Dwarf Spikerush	Eastern Lilaeopsis
Littorella	Gulf Halophila
Leafless Watermilfoil	Caribbean Halophila
Pipeworts	

Group 3.   Plants with featherlike, usually limp leaves on flexible underwater stems; stem tips often sticking out of water (pages 31-42)

Northern Watermilfoil	Eurasian Watermilfoil
Little Watermilfoil	Parrotfeather
Whorled Watermilfoil	Eastern Watermilfoil
Variable Watermilfoil	Featherfoil
Farwell Watermilfoil	Andean Watermilfoil
Marsh Mermaidweed	Southern Watermilfoil
Low Watermilfoil	

Group 4.   Plants with fine-forked, limp leaves mixed with small, roundish bladders on flexible underwater stems; flowers sticking out of water (pages 43-50)

Northern Bladderwort	Eastern Bladderwort
Flatleaf Bladderwort	Little Floating Bladderwort
Common Bladderwort	Big Floating Bladderwort
Hidden-flower Bladderwort	Dwarf Bladderwort
Purple Bladderwort	Giant Bladderwort

Group 5. Plants with clustered branches or fine-forked, bladderless, usually limp leaves on flexible underwater stems; stem tips sometimes sticking out of water (pages 51-59)

Muskgrasses, Nitellas & Tolypellas
White Water Buttercup
Yellow Water Buttercup
Coontail
Water-marigold

Lake Cress
Riverweed
Fanwort
Alga Bulrush
Limnophilas

Group 6. Plants with needlelike to oval, paired or bunched leaves on mainly flexible underwater stems; some kinds sometimes out of water (pages 60-70)

Marestail
Water-starworts
Tillaea
Horned-pondweed
Waterworts
Naiads (except Spiny Naiad)
Common Elodea
Goldenpert

Marsh-purslane
Spiny Naiad
South American Elodea
Water-purslane
Creeping Rush
Micranthemum
Mayaca

Group 7. Plants with threadlike to ribbonlike leaves scattered singly on flexible underwater stems, but often paired or bunched toward the stem tips; a few kinds also with oblong to oval floating leaves (pages 71-80)

Threadleaf Pondweed
Sago Pondweed
Widgeongrass
Bigsheath Pondweed
Slender Pondweed
Fries Pondweed
Flatstem Pondweed
Ribbonleaf Pondweed

Leafy Pondweed
Bluntleaf Pondweed
Snailseed Pondweed
Alga Pondweed
Fern Pondweed
Water-stargrass
Vasey Pondweed
Western Pondweed

Group 8. Plants with lance-shaped to oval leaves scattered singly on flexible underwater stems, but often paired or bunched toward the stem tips; some kinds also with oblong to oval floating leaves (pages 81-86)

Red Pondweed
Variable Pondweed
Whitestem Pondweed

Redhead-grass
Bigleaf Pondweed
Curly Pondweed

Group 9. Plants with lance-shaped to round floating leaves which are tapered to slightly notched at the base; some kinds also with thread-like to oval underwater leaves; and some kinds also growing partly out of water (pages 87-100)

Floating Pondweed   American Lotus
Oakes Pondweed   Upright Burhead
Water Smartweed   Longleaf Mudplantain
Marsh Smartweed   Goldenclub
Bog Pondweed   Damasonium
Watershield   Water Arrowhead (see Group 2)
Longleaf Pondweed   Watergrass
Broadleaf Waterplantain   Amphianthus
Roundleaf Bacopa   Salvinia
Heartleaf Pondweed   Ottelia

Group 10. Plants with lance-shaped to round floating leaves which are deeply notched at the base; a few kinds also growing partly out of water (pages 101-110)

Spatterdock   Roundleaf Mudplantain
Floating Caltha   Yellow Floatingheart
Northern Waterlily   American Frogbit
Northern Arrowhead   Big Floatingheart
White Waterlily   Banana Waterlily
Little Floatingheart   Blue Waterlily
European Frogbit

Group 11. Plants with coarse-toothed, lobed, or divided floating leaves; some kinds also growing partly out of water (pages 111-114)

Arctic Buttercup   Floating Buttercup
Marsileas   Lobb Buttercup
Ivyleaf Buttercup   Waterchestnut

Group 12. Little, free-floating plants (pages 115-118)

Star Duckweed   Ricciocarpus
Little Duckweeds   Water-velvets
Big Duckweeds   Eastern Wolffiella
Watermeals   Tongue Wolffiella
Riccia

Group 1. PLANTS WITH LIMP, THREADLIKE TO RIBBONLIKE LEAVES COMING UP FROM THE BOTTOM OR FROM SHORT VERTICAL STEMS; SOMETIMES PARTLY FLOATING grow in fresh inland water and in fresh to salt coastal water. The leaves are upright or nearly so in deep water, trail under or on the surface in shallow water, and sometimes are exposed on mud at low tide. Except in very young plants, the leaves vary from several inches to several feet long. Flowers are often absent.

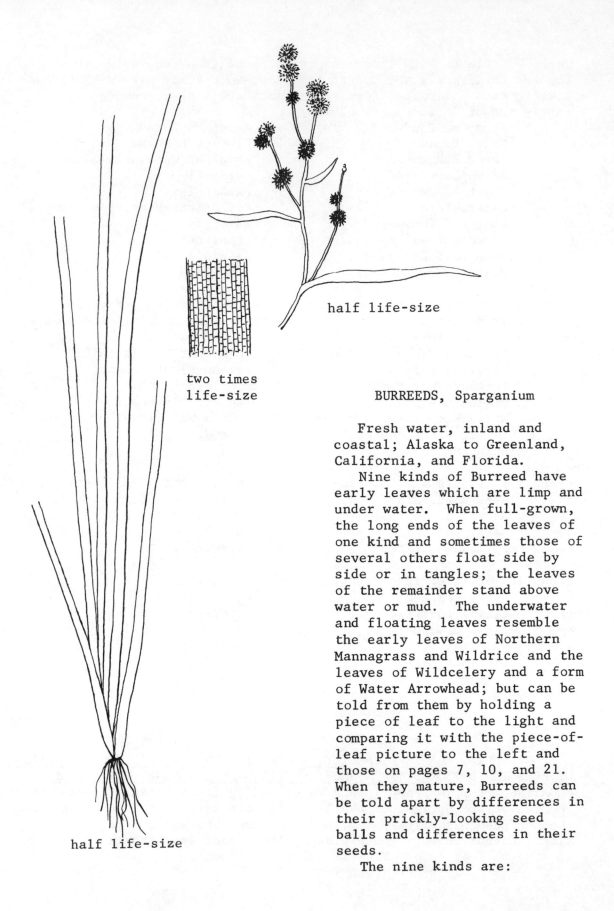

two times
life-size

half life-size

half life-size

BURREEDS, Sparganium

Fresh water, inland and
coastal; Alaska to Greenland,
California, and Florida.
Nine kinds of Burreed have
early leaves which are limp and
under water. When full-grown,
the long ends of the leaves of
one kind and sometimes those of
several others float side by
side or in tangles; the leaves
of the remainder stand above
water or mud. The underwater
and floating leaves resemble
the early leaves of Northern
Mannagrass and Wildrice and the
leaves of Wildcelery and a form
of Water Arrowhead; but can be
told from them by holding a
piece of leaf to the light and
comparing it with the piece-of-
leaf picture to the left and
those on pages 7, 10, and 21.
When they mature, Burreeds can
be told apart by differences in
their prickly-looking seed
balls and differences in their
seeds.
The nine kinds are:

6

Sparganium americanum. Ontario to Newfoundland, Texas, and Florida. Mature leaves sometimes floating.

Sparganium androcladum. Minnesota to Quebec, Oklahoma, and Virginia.

Sparganium angustifolium (Sparganium multipedunculatum and simplex). Alaska to Greenland, California, New Mexico, Minnesota, and New Jersey. Mature leaves often floating.

Sparganium chlorocarpum. Alaska to Newfoundland, California, Iowa, and North Carolina.

Sparganium eurycarpum. British Columbia to Quebec, California, Kansas, and Virginia.

Sparganium fluctuans. British Columbia to Saskatchewan and Idaho; and Minnesota to Newfoundland and Pennsylvania. Mature leaves floating.

Sparganium glomeratum. Minnesota and Quebec. Mature leaves often floating.

Sparganium hyperboreum. Alaska to Greenland, Manitoba, and Nova Scotia. Mature leaves often floating.

Sparganium minimum. Alaska to Newfoundland, New Mexico, and Pennsylvania. Mature leaves sometimes floating.

NORTHERN MANNAGRASS, Glyceria borealis

Fresh water; Alaska to Newfoundland, California, New Mexico, and Pennsylvania.

WILDRICE, Zizania aquatica

Fresh water, inland and coastal; Manitoba to Nova Scotia, Texas, and Florida; and rarely run wild from plantings in the Far West (Alberta to California).

Young plants of each kind have ribbonlike underwater leaves with long floating ends. These resemble the underwater and floating leaves of Burreeds and the leaves of Wild-celery and a form of Water Arrowhead; but can be told from them by holding a piece to the light and comparing it with the piece-of-leaf picture to the right and those on pages 6, 10, and 21. Mature plants have leafy stems which stand above water or mud.

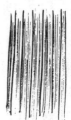

two times
life-size

7

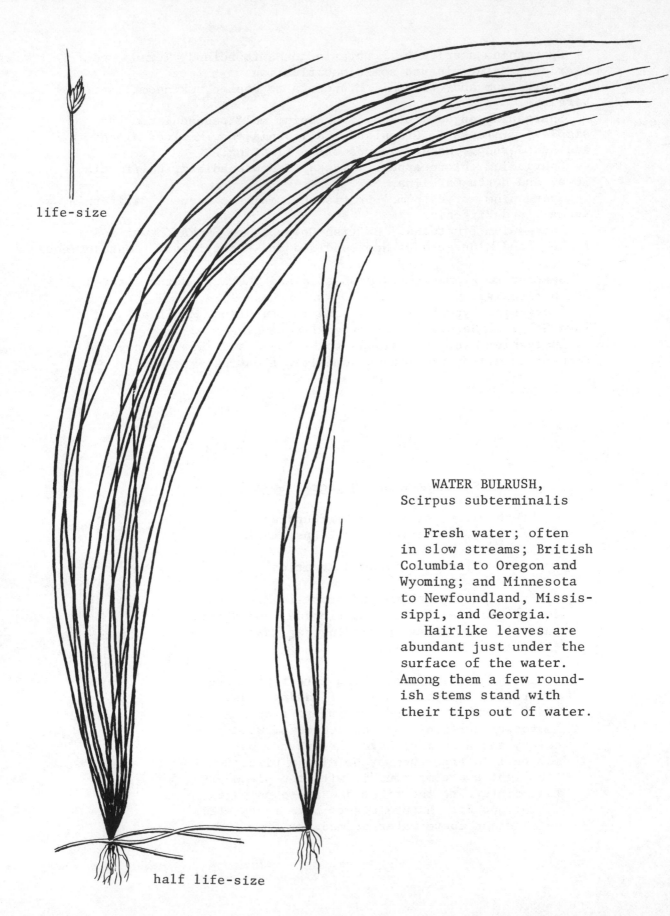

life-size

half life-size

WATER BULRUSH,
Scirpus subterminalis

Fresh water; often
in slow streams; British
Columbia to Oregon and
Wyoming; and Minnesota
to Newfoundland, Missis-
sippi, and Georgia.
Hairlike leaves are
abundant just under the
surface of the water.
Among them a few round-
ish stems stand with
their tips out of water.

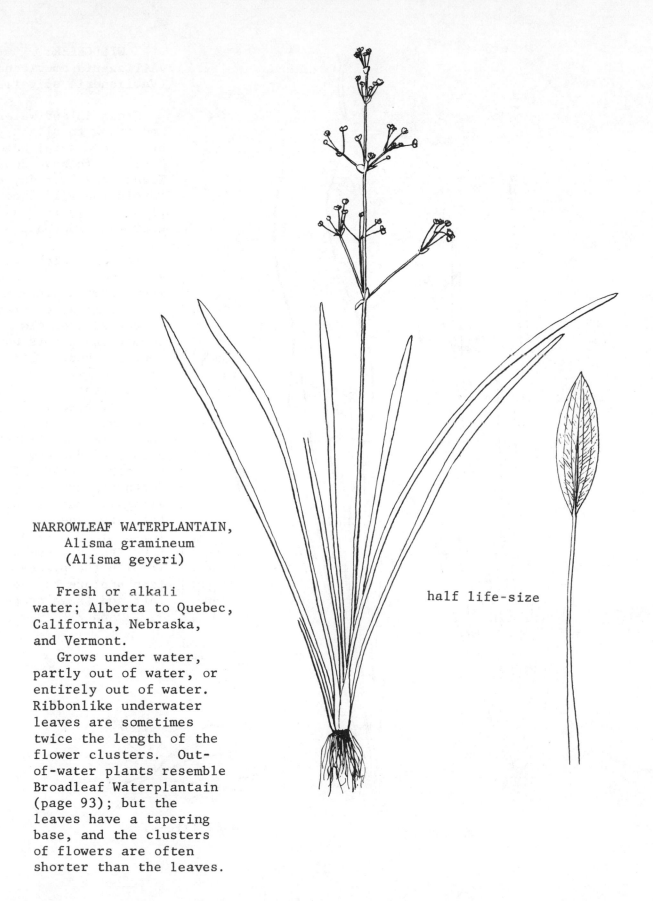

NARROWLEAF WATERPLANTAIN,
   Alisma gramineum
   (Alisma geyeri)

   Fresh or alkali
water; Alberta to Quebec,
California, Nebraska,
and Vermont.
   Grows under water,
partly out of water, or
entirely out of water.
Ribbonlike underwater
leaves are sometimes
twice the length of the
flower clusters. Out-
of-water plants resemble
Broadleaf Waterplantain
(page 93); but the
leaves have a tapering
base, and the clusters
of flowers are often
shorter than the leaves.

half life-size

9

WILDCELERY,
Vallisneria americana
(Vallisneria spiralis)

Fresh inland water and fresh to slightly brackish coastal water; Manitoba to Nova Scotia, Texas, and Florida; and rarely run wild from plantings in the Far West (Washington to Arizona).

Leaves, which are sometimes several feet long, have a fine-veined, light-colored center stripe. In summer the plants have long-stalked, cylindric pods.

The leaves resemble those of a form of Water Arrowhead, the underwater and floating leaves of Burreeds, and the early leaves of Northern Mannagrass and Wildrice; but can be told from them by holding a piece of leaf to the light and comparing it with the piece-of-leaf picture to the left and those on pages 6, 7, and 21.

two times
life-size

half life-size

half life-size

FLOWERING-RUSH,
Butomus umbellatus

Not pictured.
   A native of Europe which
was discovered along the
tidal St. Lawrence River
about 1900 and now grows in
fresh water in Idaho; and
Michigan to Quebec, Illi-
nois, and Vermont.
   Usually stands above
shallow water or mud, with
knee-high or higher narrow,
upright leaves surrounding
a stalk topped with a loose
cluster of pink, 6-parted
flowers. These are about
3/4 inch across.
   In deeper water, has only
limp leaves which do not
reach above the surface.
These resemble the leaves
of Burreeds and Wildcelery,
but are usually narrower
and less translucent and
appear less veiny (see the
piece-of-leaf pictures on
pages 6 and 10).

EELGRASS, Zostera marina

   Salt water; Alaska to
California; and Hudson Bay
to North Carolina.
   Often in dense beds in
soft-bottomed bays. Some
bays are so shallow that
most of the water drains
out at low tide; and for a
while the ribbonlike
foliage is left sprawling
on the mud. Seeds are half-
hidden in a long row in
leaf sheaths.
   Narrow-leaved plants
resemble Shoalgrass (page
12), with which it grows in
North Carolina; but Eelgrass
leaves have a roundish tip.

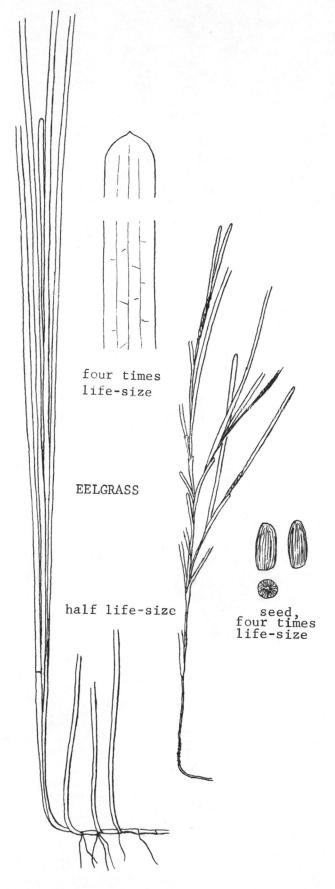

four times
life-size

EELGRASS

half life-size

seed,
four times
life-size

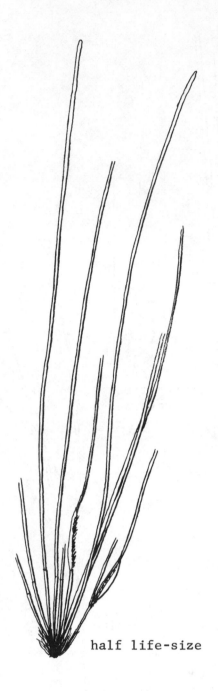

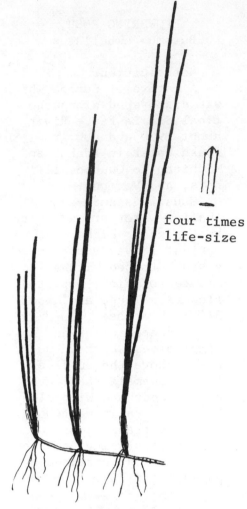

four times
life-size

half life-size

half life-size

SURFGRASS, Phyllospadix scouleri
(Phyllospadix torreyi)

Salt water; British Columbia
to California.
   Flowers are sometimes in
several clusters on a much longer
stalk than the ones pictured.

SHOALGRASS, Halodule wrightii

Salt water; North Caro-
lina; and Texas to Florida.
   Leaves flat in cross-
section. Flowers scarce.
   Resembles narrow-leaved
plants of Eelgrass (page 11),
with which it grows in North
Carolina; but has a 3-pointed
leaf tip which could be mis-
taken for a broken end. Resembles Manateegrass (page 13);
but has flat leaves with a
3-pointed tip.

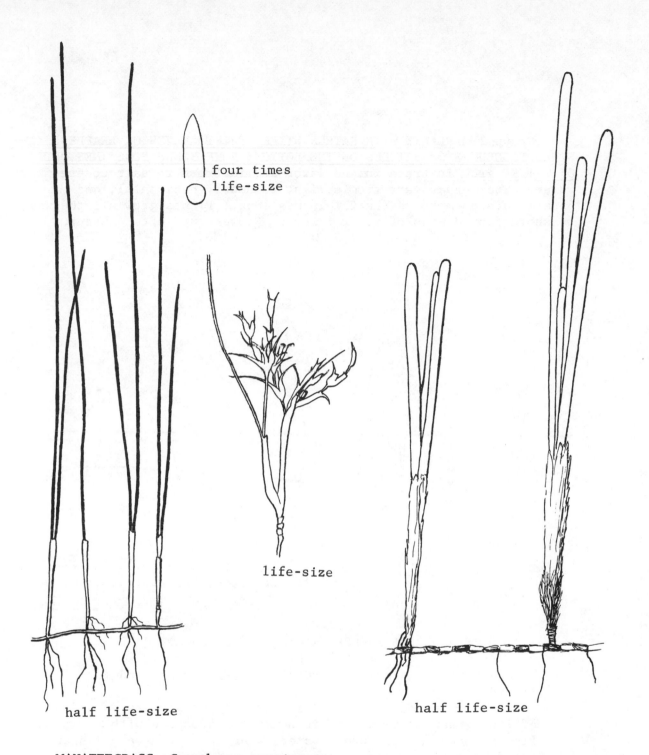

four times
life-size

life-size

half life-size

half life-size

MANATEEGRASS, Cymodocea manatorum

Salt water; Texas to Florida.
Leaves round in cross-section.
Flowers common.
Resembles Shoalgrass (page 12);
but has round leaves with a blunt
tip.

TURTLEGRASS,
Thalassia testudinum

Salt water; Texas
to Florida.

13

Group 2. <u>PLANTS WITH RATHER STIFF, SHORT LEAVES OR LEAFLESS</u>
<u>STEMS IN CLUMPS OR PATCHES ON THE BOTTOM; SOME KINDS SOMETIMES OUT</u>
<u>OF WATER</u> grow in fresh inland water and in fresh to salt coastal
water. The leaves vary from upright to nearly horizontal, and
usually are no more than a few inches long. Plants grow all the way
to shore from depths of several feet. Flowers are often absent.

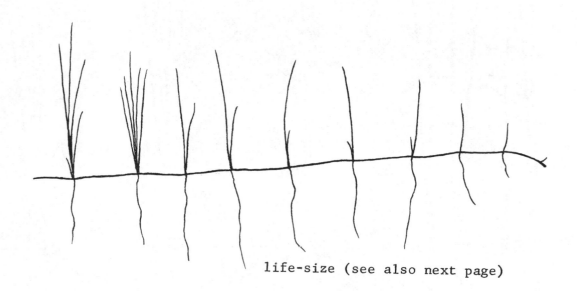

life-size (see also next page)

SLENDER SPIKERUSH, Eleocharis acicularis

    Fresh water; Alaska to Greenland, California, and
Florida.
    Usually on wet shores and in marshes, growing as a turf
of fine green stems which, in summer, are topped with brown
flower heads. Often under water, where the stems are longer
and do not bloom. In streams, displaced rootstocks sometimes trail and produce still longer stems.
    Resembles Dwarf Spikerush (page 23); but Slender Spikerush
has thinner stems and is not known to produce tubers or to
grow in brackish coastal marshes.

14

SLENDER SPIKERUSH, life-size
(see also preceding page)

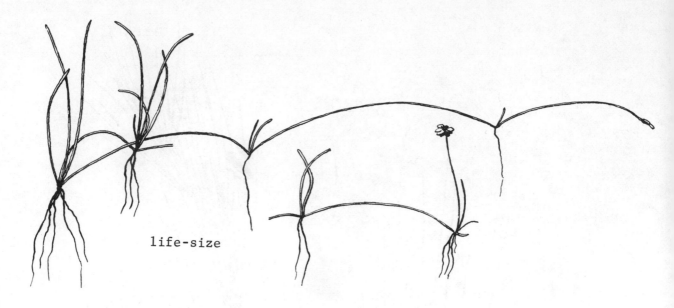

life-size

CREEPING BUTTERCUP, Ranunculus flammula
(Ranunculus reptans)

    Fresh water; Alaska to Greenland, California, New Mexico, Minnesota, and Pennsylvania.
    Grows either under water or on wet shores. Leaves are connected by above-ground runners. Out-of-water plants have yellow flowers.

QUILLWORTS, Isoetes

half life-size

    Fresh inland water and fresh to slightly brackish coastal water; Alaska to Greenland, California, and Florida.
    Quillworts resemble each other so much that they can be told apart only by using a microscope to look at the markings on spores pocketed in the base of leaves. Thirteen kinds vary considerably in size, number of leaves, and stiffness of leaves (sometimes they are long and limp); but some vary almost as much within themselves. Occasionally they grow partly or entirely out of water.
    The thirteen kinds are:

Isoetes bolanderi. British Columbia to Alberta, California, Arizona, and Colorado.

Isoetes eatoni. New Hampshire to New Jersey.

Isoetes engelmanni. Missouri to New Hampshire, Alabama, and Georgia.

Isoetes flaccida. Georgia and Florida.

Isoetes foveolata. New Hampshire to Connecticut.

Isoetes howellii. Washington to Montana and California.

Isoetes macrospora. Minnesota to Newfoundland and Virginia.

Isoetes melanopoda (Isoetes butleri, melanospora, and virginica). South Dakota to Virginia, Texas, and Georgia.

Isoetes muricata (Isoetes braunii). Alaska to Greenland, California, Colorado, Minnesota, and New Jersey.

Isoetes nuttallii (Isoetes orcuttii). Washington to Idaho and California.

Isoetes occidentalis. Washington to Colorado and California.

Isoetes riparia (Isoetes saccharata). Michigan to Newfoundland and North Carolina.

Isoetes tuckermani. Quebec to Newfoundland, New York, and Connecticut.

The smaller Quillworts resemble Littorella (page 23) and Pillwort (page 28); but Quillwort leaves have a much-enlarged base, and clumps of leaves are not connected by rootstocks. The smaller Quillworts resemble Pipeworts (page 25); but Quillwort leaves taper only a little from the much-enlarged base, and their roots are not closely crosslined.

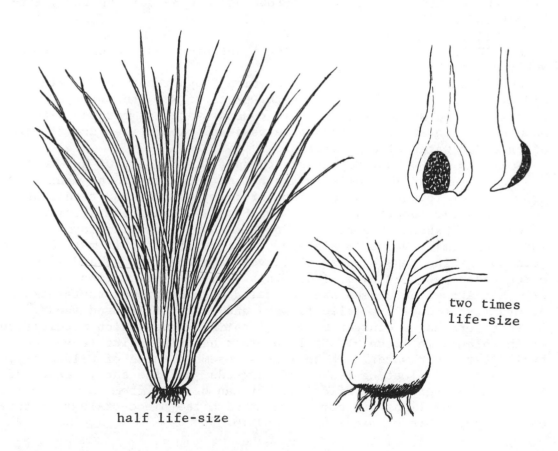

half life-size

two times
life-size

life-size

SUBULARIA, Subularia aquatica

Fresh water; Alaska to Quebec, California,
Utah, Minnesota, and New York.
Has tiny white flowers and roundish pods,
either under water or on wet shores.
Resembles the underwater form of Bog Rush
(page 26); but the clumps of leaves are not
connected by underground rootstocks, and
plants often have flowers or seed pods.

ARROWHEADS, Sagittaria

Fresh water, inland and coastal; Alaska to Quebec, California, and
Florida.
Young plants of five kinds of Arrowhead often grow under water as
clumps of narrow, stalkless leaves. The leaves may be stiff or limp,
short or ribbonlike, blunt-tipped or sharp-tipped, flat or as-thick-as-
wide. When they mature, these Arrowheads can be told apart by their
leaves and seeds.
The five kinds are:
BUR ARROWHEAD, Sagittaria rigida. Not pictured. Manitoba to Quebec,
Nebraska, Alabama, and Virginia.
HOODED ARROWHEAD, Sagittaria calycina (Lophotocarpus calycinus and
spongiosus). California; and South Dakota to New Brunswick, New Mexico,
Louisiana, and North Carolina. In coastal water it matures without
much change in shape or size of leaves; and the foliage and flowers are
often under water at high tide.
NORTHERN ARROWHEAD, Sagittaria cuneata (see pages 104 and 105).
SLENDER ARROWHEAD, Sagittaria graminea (Sagittaria chapmanii,
cristata, cycloptera, eatoni, isoetiformis, macrocarpa, teres, and
weatherbiana). South Dakota to Nova Scotia, Texas, and Florida.
WATER ARROWHEAD, Sagittaria subulata (Sagittaria filiformis, lorata,
and stagnorum). Maine to Alabama. In coastal water it matures without
much change in shape or size of leaves; and the foliage and flowers are
often under water at high tide. This form resembles Limosella (page
22); but Arrowhead clumps are connected by underground rootstocks and
eventually produce 3-petaled flowers and balls of exposed seeds.
Another form has a cluster of oval floating leaves which resemble some
of the plants in Group 9. Still another has ribbonlike leaves which
trail just under water. These leaves resemble those of Wildcelery, the
underwater and floating leaves of Burreeds, and the early leaves of
Northern Mannagrass and Wildrice; but can be told from them by holding
a piece to the light and comparing it with the piece-of-leaf picture on
page 21 and those on pages 6, 7, and 10.

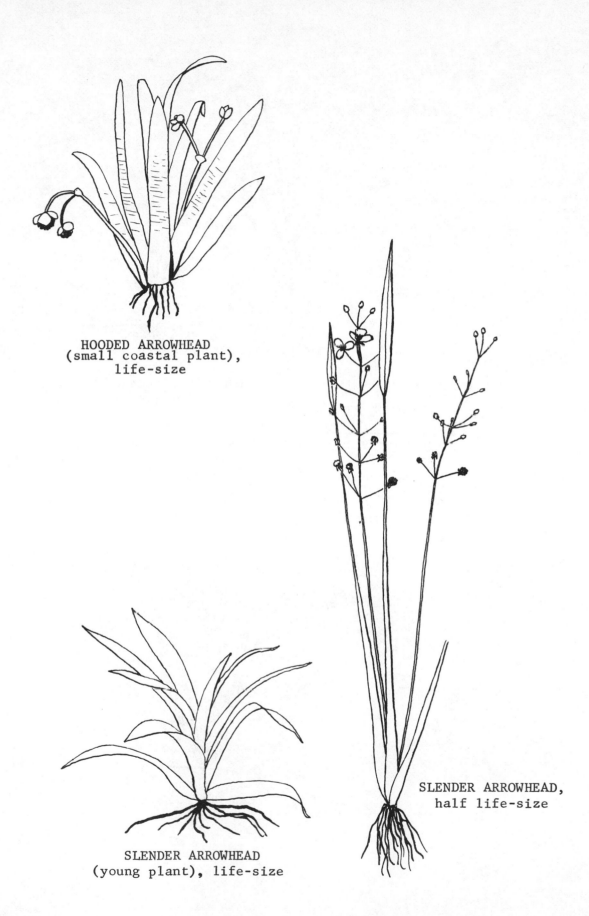

HOODED ARROWHEAD
(small coastal plant),
life-size

SLENDER ARROWHEAD,
half life-size

SLENDER ARROWHEAD
(young plant), life-size

WATER ARROWHEAD (coastal **plants**),
life-size

WATER ARROWHEAD (floating-leaved),
half life-size

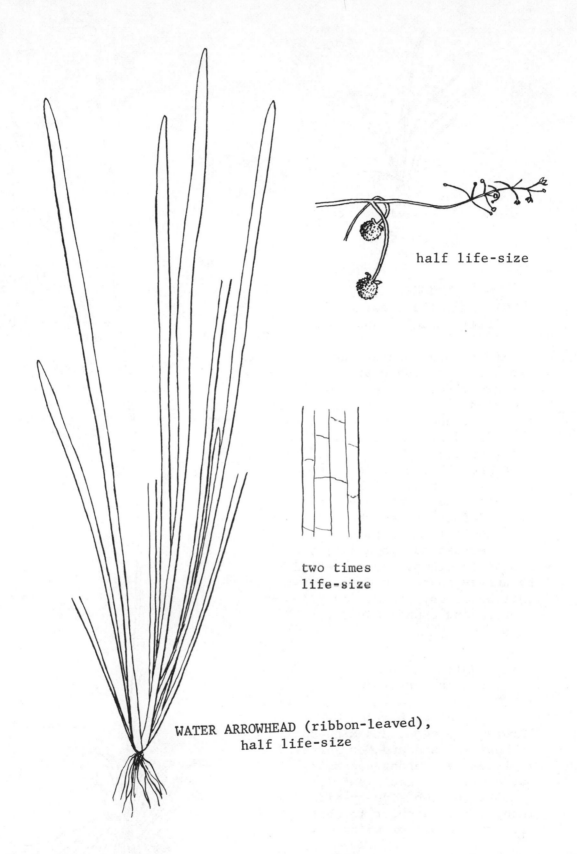

half life-size

two times
life-size

WATER ARROWHEAD (ribbon-leaved),
half life-size

21

life-size

LIMOSELLA,
Limosella aquatica
(Limosella acaulis and subulata)

Fresh inland water and
fresh to brackish coastal water;
Northwest Territories to Newfoundland, California, New Mexico,
Missouri, and North Carolina (but
not inland east of the Mississippi River).
  Along the coast, is under
water at high tide. Inland, has
long-stalked, oval leaves and
grows mainly on wet shores.
  Resembles small plants of
Water Arrowhead (page 20); but
Limosella clumps are connected
by above-ground runners, and
they have tiny, 5-petaled
flowers and roundish pods.

WATER LOBELIA,
Lobelia dortmanna

Fresh water; British Co-
lumbia to Oregon; and Minnesota
to Newfoundland and New Jersey.
  Leaves are under water or
out of water. Each leaf is
composed of two side-by-side
tubes. The lavender to white
flowers are out of water.

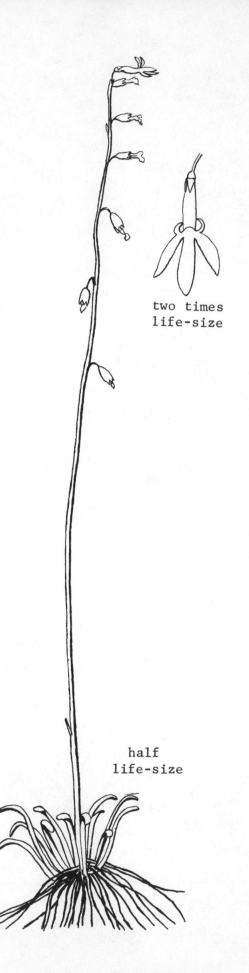

two times
life-size

half
life-size

DWARF SPIKERUSH
Eleocharis parvula
(Scirpus nanus, Eleocharis coloradoensis)

Fresh, brackish, and alkali inland water and fresh to brackish coastal water; British Columbia to Newfoundland, California, and Florida (but very rare inland east of the Mississippi River).

Usually on wet shores and in marshes, growing as a turf of fine green stems which, in summer, are topped with green or brownish flower heads. Often under water in fresh to brackish pools and bays along the coasts, where the stems do not bloom. In summer and fall the rootstocks produce tiny tubers.

Resembles Slender Spikerush (pages 14 and 15); but has thicker stems, produces tubers, and is common in brackish coastal marshes.

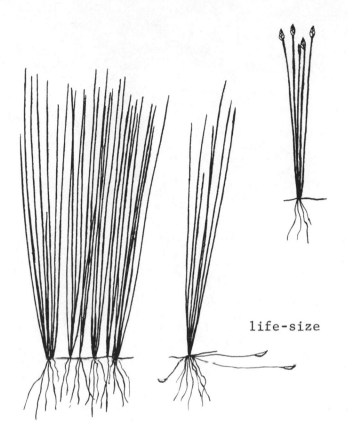

life-size

LITTORELLA,
Littorella uniflora
(Littorella americana)

Fresh water; Ontario to Newfoundland, Minnesota, and New York.

Grows in water to several feet deep, or on shore; but blooms only out of water.

Resembles small Quillworts (page 16) and Pipeworts (page 25); but the clumps are connected by rootstocks.

life-size

23

LEAFLESS WATERMILFOIL,
Myriophyllum tenellum

   Fresh water; Minne-
sota to Newfoundland and
Virginia.
   Stems have a few,
barely visible leaves.
Flowers are on stems
which stand above water.
   The Watermilfoils
with featherlike under-
water leaves are de-
scribed on pages 31-42.

life-size

PIPEWORTS, Eriocaulon

There are two kinds of
Pipewort which grow with
leaves under water and
flower heads sticking out,
or with the whole plant out
of water. Their thin
leaves taper from a wide
base to a threadlike tip
and are checkerboarded with
fine veins. Their roots
have crosslines which make
them look like tiny, whitish angleworms. They are:
EARLY PIPEWORT,
Eriocaulon compressum.
Fresh water; New Jersey to
Texas. Leaves usually
larger than those of Northern Pipewort, and heads
usually maturing earlier.
NORTHERN PIPEWORT,
Eriocaulon septangulare
(Eriocaulon lineare and
parkeri). Fresh water,
inland and coastal;
Minnesota to Newfoundland,
Alabama, and Florida.
Resembles Littorella (page
23), with which it often
grows; but clumps of Pipewort leaves are not con-
nected by rootstocks, and
Pipewort roots are closely
crosslined. Resembles the
smaller Quillworts (page
16); but Pipewort leaves
taper conspicuously from a
wide base, and their roots
are closely crosslined.

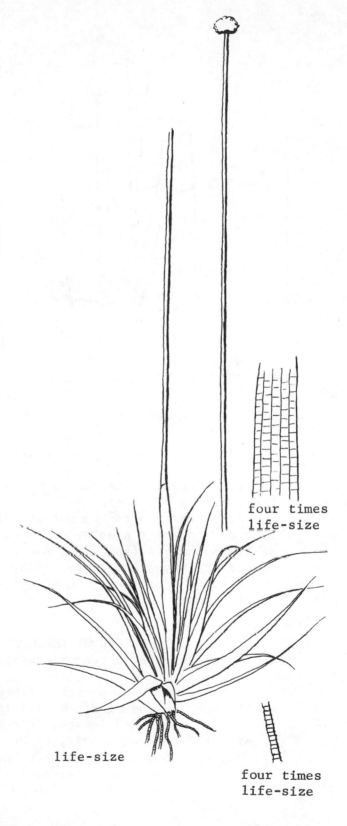

four times
life-size

life-size

four times
life-size

25

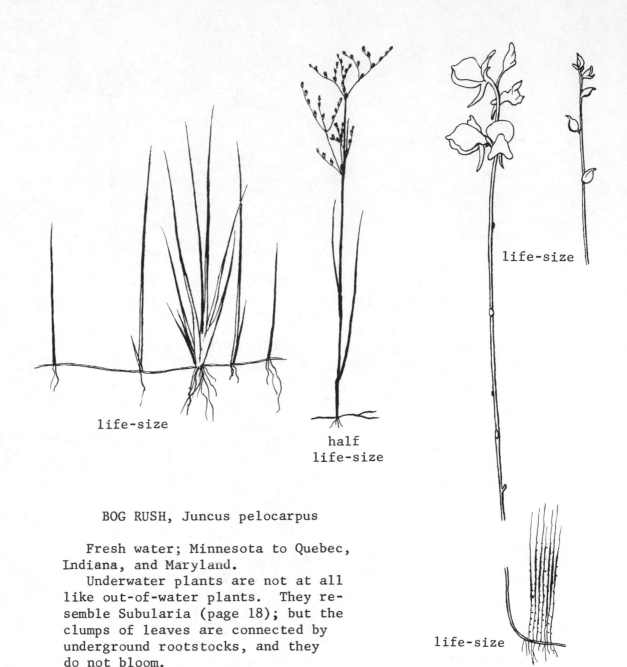

life-size

half
life-size

life-size

life-size

BOG RUSH, Juncus pelocarpus

   Fresh water; Minnesota to Quebec,
Indiana, and Maryland.
   Underwater plants are not at all
like out-of-water plants. They resemble Subularia (page 18); but the
clumps of leaves are connected by
underground rootstocks, and they
do not bloom.

HORNED BLADDERWORT, Utricularia cornuta
(Utricularia juncea; Stomoisia cornuta, juncea, and virgatula)

   Fresh water; Minnesota to Newfoundland, Texas, and Florida
(but not in the Middle Mississippi Valley).
   Slim undivided leaves, fringed with speck-sized bladders,
are half-buried in soil, either under water or out of water.
They are likely to be overlooked until the turf beneath flowers
is dug out and the soil carefully washed away. Flowers vary from
big, open, and bright yellow to small and permanently budlike.

ZIGZAG BLADDERWORT,
     Utricularia subulata
(Setiscapella cleistogama and
subulata)

     Fresh water; Ontario to
Nova Scotia, Texas, and Florida.
     Tiny undivided leaves are
half-buried in soil, either
under water or out of water.
They are likely to be overlooked
until the turf beneath flowers
is dug out and the soil carefully washed away. Speck-sized
bladders are on underground
branches. Flowers vary from
open and yellow to permanently
budlike.

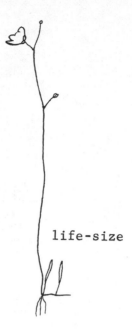

life-size

LAVENDER BLADDERWORT,
Utricularia resupinata
(Lecticula resupinata)

     Fresh water; Wisconsin
to Nova Scotia, Indiana, and
Delaware; and Georgia and
Florida.
     Slim undivided leaves,
fringed with a few speck-
sized bladders, are half-
buried in soil, either under
water or out of water. They
are likely to be overlooked
until the turf beneath flowers is dug out and the soil
carefully washed away. Has
one lavender flower to a
stem.

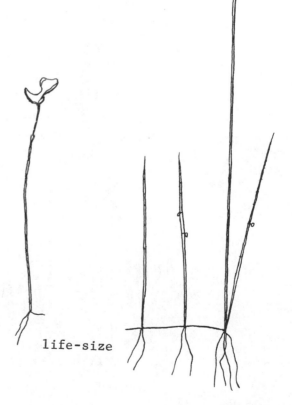

life-size

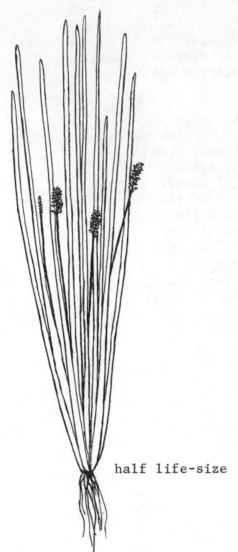

FLOWERING-QUILLWORT,
Lilaea scilloides

Fresh water; British
Columbia to Alberta,
California, and Montana
(but commonest in cen-
tral California).
 Varies from one-
quarter the height
pictured to twice as
high.

half life-size

PILLWORT, Pilularia americana

 In open-land depressions
which contain water in the
spring; Oregon and California;
and Kansas to Georgia and
Texas.
 Leaf tips uncoil as they
mature. Spores are borne in
fuzzy balls at the base of
leaves.
 Resembles small Quillworts
(page 16); but Pillwort
clumps are connected by rootstocks, and Pillwort leaves do
not have enlarged bases.

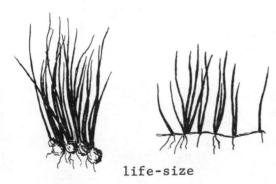

life-size

WESTERN LILAEOPSIS,
Lilaeopsis occidentalis

Fresh to brackish
coastal water; British
Columbia to California.
   Under water at high
tide, out of water at
low. Leaves are hollow
and jointed. Flowers
are tiny and white.

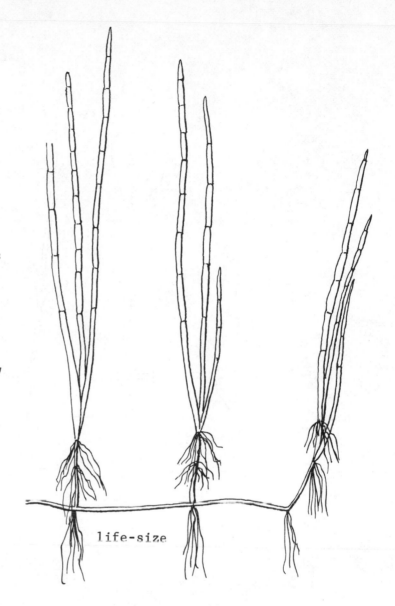

life-size

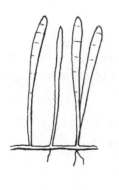 

life-size

EASTERN LILAEOPSIS, Lilaeopsis chinensis
(Lilaeopsis lineata)

   Fresh to brackish coastal water; Nova
Scotia to Louisiana.
   Under water at high tide, out of
water at low. Leaves are hollow and
jointed. Flowers are tiny and white.

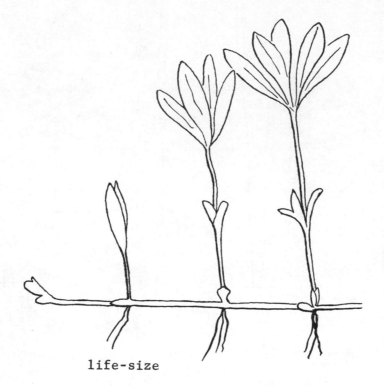

GULF HALOPHILA,
Halophila engelmanni

Salt water;
Florida and Texas.
Firm leaves are
stalkless or short-
stalked and have a
faint midvein.

life-size

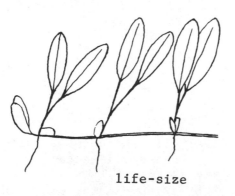

CARIBBEAN HALOPHILA,
Halophila baillonis

Salt water; Florida.
Limp leaves are long-stalked
and have a conspicuous midvein.

life-size

30

Group 3. <u>PLANTS WITH FEATHERLIKE, USUALLY LIMP LEAVES ON</u>
<u>FLEXIBLE UNDERWATER STEMS; STEM TIPS OFTEN STICKING OUT OF WATER</u>
grow in fresh inland water and in fresh to brackish coastal water.
The stems vary from upright to horizontal and from a foot long to
several feet; and they are usually branched. The underwater leaves
usually collapse when taken out of water. At low tide, Eurasian
Watermilfoil reaches the surface in a tangle of horizontal stems.
When water levels drop in summer, several other kinds make a similar
tangle; and a few produce short out-of-water stems. Most Watermilfoils are hard to tell apart when they don't have flowers or seeds.
When in bloom, most of them have tiny brownish flowers in spikes
which stand above the water. When the seeds are ripe, the spikes are
usually lying in water. The seeds are partly joined to each other in
fours. The largest kinds are only a little more than 1/16 inch long.

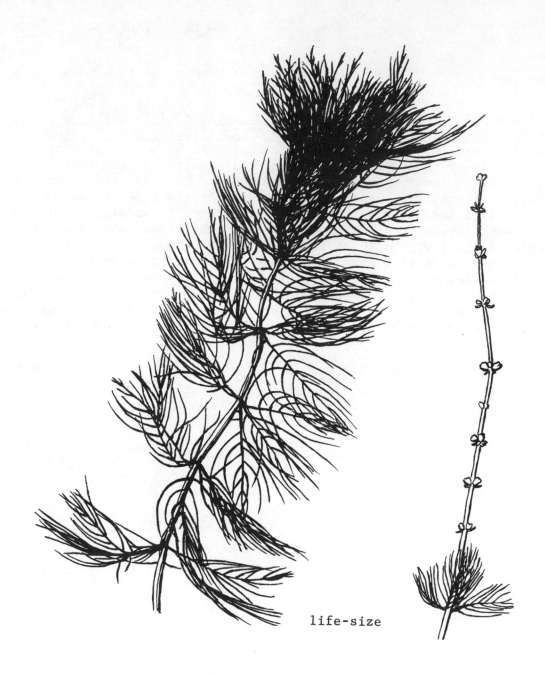

life-size

NORTHERN WATERMILFOIL, Myriophyllum exalbescens
(Myriophyllum magdalenense)

Fresh water, inland and rarely coastal; Alaska to Baffin Island,
California, Kansas, and Pennsylvania.
Leaves often not collapsing when taken out of water, and often
coated with lime.
Resembles Whorled (page 34), Eurasian (page 38), and Little (page 33)
Watermilfoils, with which it sometimes grows. Its joints are farther
apart than those of Whorled; therefore the usually buff or pinkish
stems are not hidden by leaves. Its leaves have fewer, wider-spaced
leaflets than those of Eurasian. Its stems and leaves are usually
twice as large as those of Little.

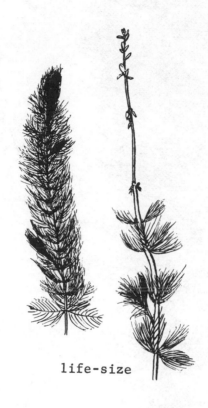

life-size

LITTLE WATERMILFOIL, Myriophyllum alterniflorum

   Fresh water, inland and rarely coastal; Alaska
to Newfoundland, Wisconsin, and Connecticut.
   The leaves are so small and close together
that a person has to look closely to be sure they
are featherlike.
   Resembles Northern (page 32) and Whorled (page
34) Watermilfoils; but stems and leaves are
usually no more than half the size of theirs,
and upper flowers are scattered instead of in
whorls.

33

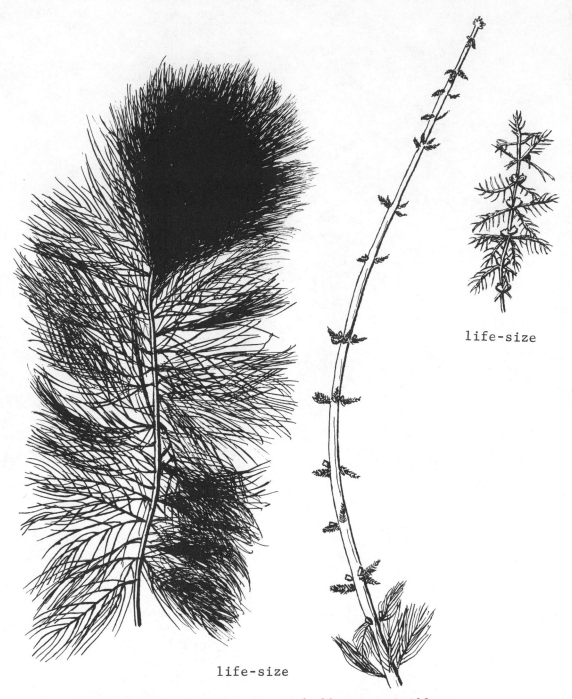

life-size

life-size

life-size

WHORLED WATERMILFOIL, Myriophyllum verticillatum

Fresh water, inland and rarely coastal; Alaska to Newfoundland,
California, Illinois, and New Jersey.
    Stems usually green and almost hidden by leaves. During low water
in summer, patches of short out-of-water stems sometimes grow on mud.
    Resembles Northern (page 32), Eurasian (page 38), Little (page 33),
and Farwell (page 36) Watermilfoils, with which it sometimes grows.
Its joints are closer together than those of Northern; therefore its
usually green stems are nearly hidden by leaves. Its leaves have
fewer leaflets than those of Eurasian. Its stems and leaves are
usually twice as large as those of Little. Its out-of-water flowers
contrast with Farwell's underwater ones.

34

VARIABLE WATERMILFOIL, Myriophyllum heterophyllum (Myriophyllum hippuroides)

Fresh water; British Columbia to New Brunswick, California, and Florida.
Stems, stouter than in most other Watermilfoils, are thickly covered with limp leaves. Spikes, also stouter than in most of the others, are usually thickly covered with firm, oval to linear leaves.

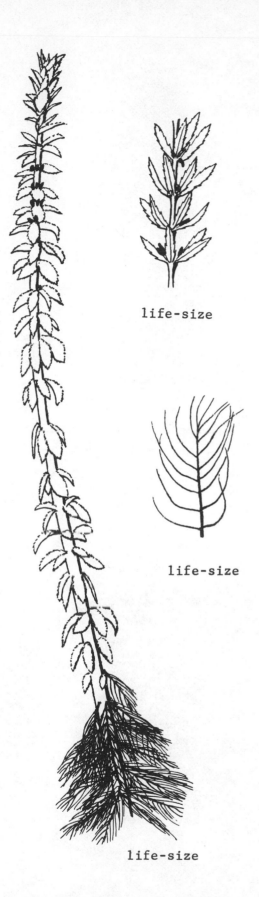

life-size

life-size

life-size

35

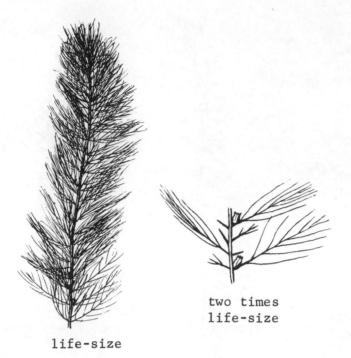

FARWELL WATERMILFOIL,
Myriophyllum farwellii

Fresh water; Minne-
sota to Nova Scotia and
Vermont.
Flowers all at the
base of underwater
leaves, not in out-of-
water spikes.
Resembles Whorled
Watermilfoil (page 34),
with which it sometimes
grows; but Farwell's
flowers are at the base
of underwater leaves.

two times
life-size

life-size

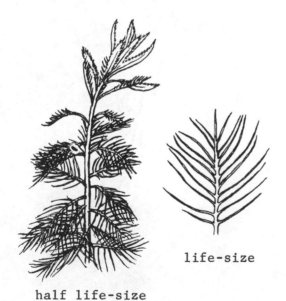

MARSH MERMAIDWEED,
Proserpinaca palustris
(Proserpinaca amblyogona and
platycarpa)

Fresh water; Wisconsin to
Nova Scotia, Texas, and
Florida.
From fall to early spring,
stems of the preceding year
send out underwater stems with
foliage resembling that of
Northern Watermilfoil (page
32), except that there is only
one leaf at a joint. By mid-
spring, stem tips with toothed
leaves reach out of water. In
summer, the whole plant is
often out of water and there
is a three-cornered seed at
the base of many of the leaves.

life-size

half life-size

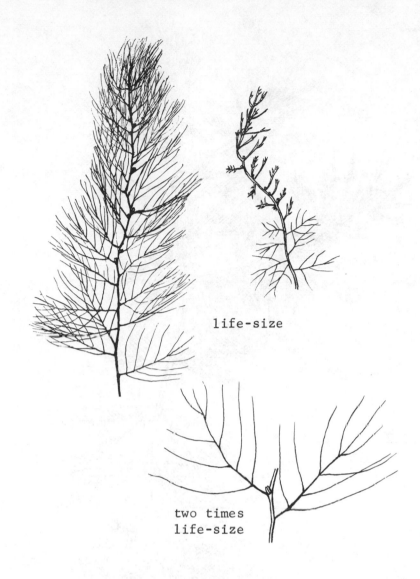

life-size

two times
life-size

LOW WATERMILFOIL, Myriophyllum humile

Fresh water, inland and rarely coastal; Nova Scotia to
North Carolina.

Stems thinly covered with very fine, limp leaves;
their tip sometimes out of water and bearing small, firm,
slightly-divided or undivided leaves. Usually there is only
one out-of-water leaf at a joint. Flowers are at the base
of either underwater leaves or out-of-water leaves. During
low water in summer, patches of short out-of-water stems
sometimes grow on mud.

Foliage on underwater stems resembles that of Eastern
Watermilfoil (page 40), with which it sometimes grows; but
Low Watermilfoil has smooth-backed seeds which are 1/32
inch long or a little more--so tiny that they are easily
overlooked.

37

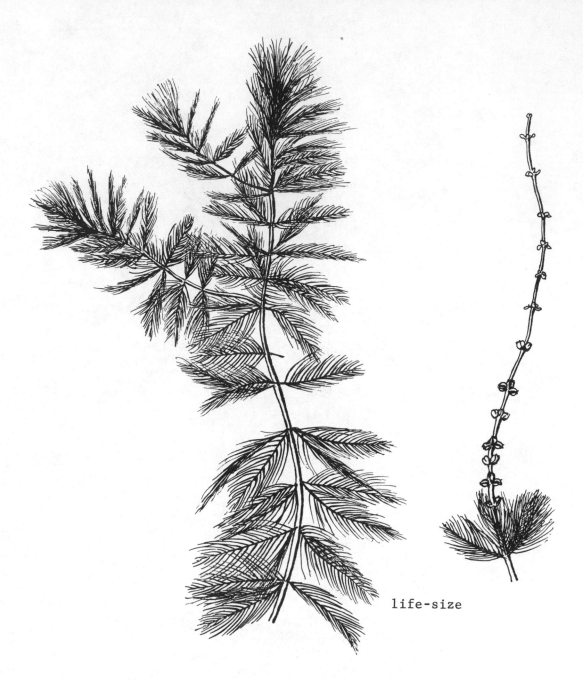

life-size

EURASIAN WATERMILFOIL, Myriophyllum spicatum

Fresh inland water and fresh to brackish coastal water; California;
and Wisconsin to Vermont, Texas, and Florida.

This plant has been in the United States for at least seventy years.
Since 1955 it has become very abundant in Upper Chesapeake Bay, the
tidal Potomac River, and several Tennessee Valley reservoirs.

Leaves look like weatherbeaten feathers because of their 12-16 pairs
of close-together leaflets.

Resembles Northern (page 32) and Whorled (page 34) Watermilfoils,
with which it sometimes grows; but can be told from them by its more
featherlike leaves.

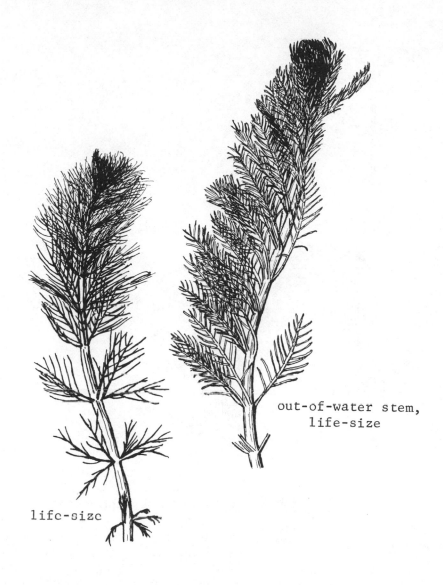

out-of-water stem,
life-size

life-size

PARROTFEATHER, Myriophyllum brasiliense
(Myriophyllum proserpinacoides)

A native of South America which is a common aquarium
plant and which has run wild in fresh water from Idaho to
California and Arizona; and Kansas to New York, Texas,
and Florida.
Differs from other Watermilfoils in having firm, grayish-
green foliage which pushes a few inches out of water. Has
some underwater branches with limp leaves.

two times
life-size

life-size

EASTERN WATERMILFOIL,
Myriophyllum pinnatum

Fresh water, inland and coastal;
Iowa to Massachusetts, Texas, and
Florida.

Stems thinly covered with very fine,
limp leaves; their tip often out of
water and bearing small, firm, slightly-
divided leaves. Out-of-water leaves
usually clustered at joints and with
a flower at their base. During low
water in summer, patches of short out-
of-water stems sometimes grow on mud.

Foliage on underwater stems resembles that of Low Watermilfoil (page 37),
with which it sometimes grows; but
Eastern has rough-backed seeds which
are 1/16 inch long.

40

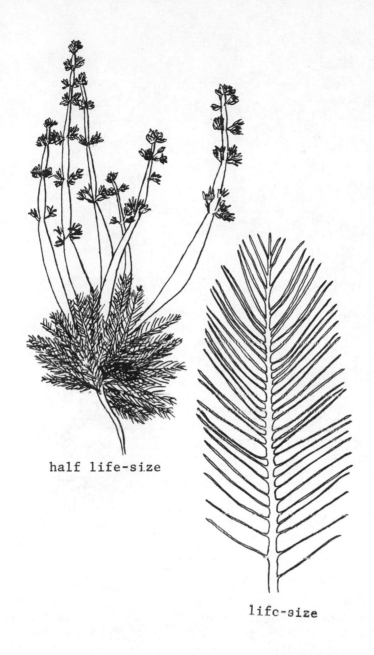

half life-size

life-size

FEATHERFOIL, Hottonia inflata

Usually in pools in freshwater swamps; Missouri
to Maine, Texas, and Florida.
Comes up from seed in the fall; and from fall to
spring the leaves are bunched toward the tip of
unbranched stems, just below the surface of the
water. Usually is overlooked until clusters of
swollen flower stalks grow above water in spring
and early summer.

41

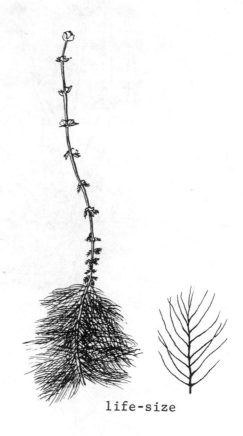

life-size   life-size

ANDEAN WATERMILFOIL,
Myriophyllum elatinoides

   A native of South
America and New Zealand
which has run wild in the
Deschutes River near Bend,
Oregon.
   Out-of-water leaves
grayish-green. Midvein of
underwater leaves tapering
from base to tip.

SOUTHERN WATERMILFOIL,
Myriophyllum laxum

   Fresh water; North
Carolina to Alabama.
   Resembles Whorled Watermilfoil (page 34) which has
not been found south of New
Jersey. Resembles Variable
Watermilfoil (page 35); but
has slimmer stems and
nearly leafless spikes.

Group 4. <u>PLANTS WITH FINE-FORKED, LIMP LEAVES MIXED WITH SMALL</u>
<u>ROUNDISH BLADDERS ON FLEXIBLE UNDERWATER STEMS; FLOWERS STICKING OUT</u>
<u>OF WATER</u> are most abundant in brownish, shallow, fresh water over
bottoms mushy with decaying vegetation. The stems grow horizontally
or slantwise; vary from an inch long in Dwarf Bladderwort to twenty
feet in Giant Bladderwort; and are usually branched. The leaves
collapse when taken out of water. Some kinds are hard to tell apart
when they don't have flowers. When in bloom, their yellow, purplish,
or whitish flowers are on out-of-water stalks.

Bladderworts which do not have forked underwater leaves are
described on pages 26 and 27.

NORTHERN BLADDERWORT,
    Utricularia minor

Fresh water; Alaska to
Greenland, California, Colorado, and Pennsylvania.
    Bladders and green
leaves are mixed together.
The leaves fork into
flattish, very-sharp-tipped
leaflets. Flowers are
yellow.

life-size   two times
                   life-size

43

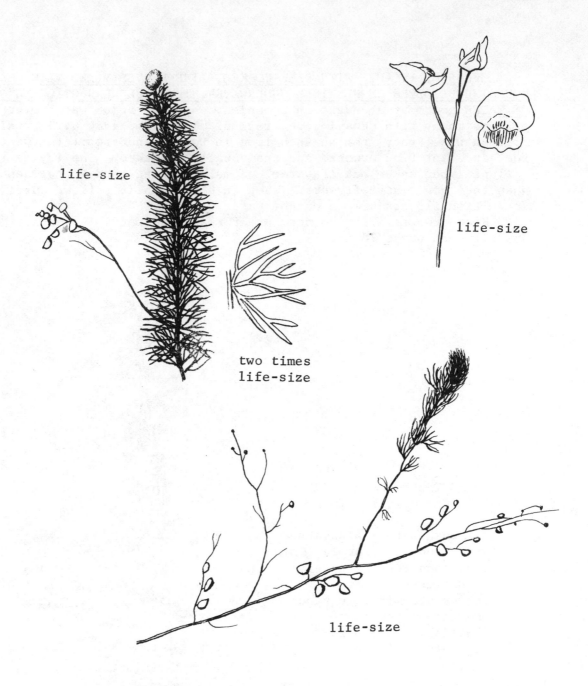

life-size

two times
life-size

life-size

life-size

FLATLEAF BLADDERWORT, Utricularia intermedia
(Utricularia ochroleuca)

Fresh water; Alaska to Greenland, California, and New Jersey.
Has two kinds of branches. One is thickly covered with green
leaves which fork into flattish, usually blunt-tipped leaflets.
The other has scattered, colorless to blackish bladders. Flowers
are yellow.

44

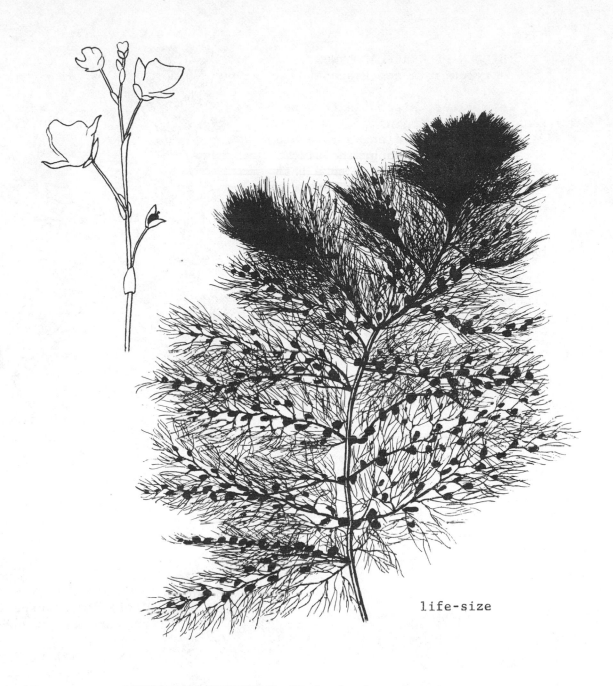

life-size

COMMON BLADDERWORT, Utricularia vulgaris
(Utricularia macrorhiza)

    Fresh water; Alaska to Newfoundland, California, Arkansas, and
North Carolina.
    Flowers are yellow.
    Foliage resembles that of Hidden-flower (page 46), Little Floating
(page 48), and Big Floating (page 49) Bladderworts. The leaves are
usually much larger and more forked than those of Hidden-flower, and
they have larger bladders. The leaves have less zigzag forking and
larger bladders than Little Floating. The leaves have less zigzag
forking than Big Floating.

HIDDEN-FLOWER BLADDERWORT,
Utricularia geminiscapa

Fresh water; Wisconsin to Newfoundland and Virginia.

Here and there along a main stem
are globular pods about the size of
a bladder, on a stalk no more than
1/2 inch long. These develop from
petal-less flowers.

Resembles small plants of Common
Bladderwort (page 45); but Hidden-
flower's leaves are usually less-
forked, its bladders are usually
smaller, and its petal-bearing
flowers are much smaller.

two times
life-size

two times
life-size

life-size

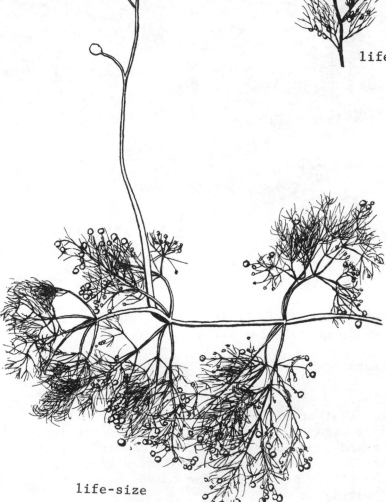

PURPLE BLADDERWORT,
Utricularia purpurea
(Vesiculina purpurea)

Fresh water; Wis-
consin to Nova Scotia,
Texas, and Florida
(but not in the Middle
Mississippi Valley).

The only Bladder-
wort with a cluster of
branches at each joint
of its stems. Flowers
are purplish.

life-size

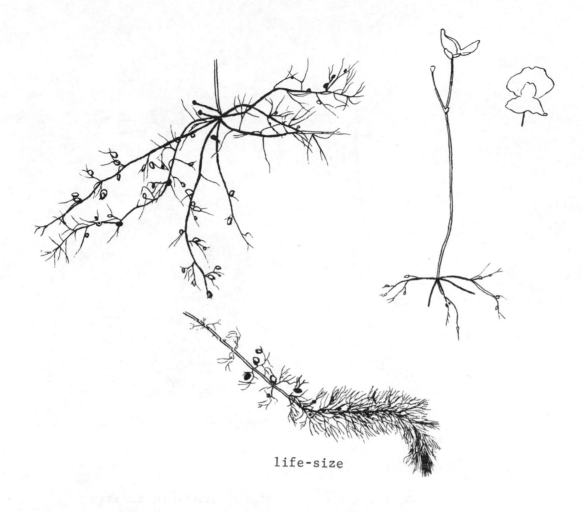

life-size

EASTERN BLADDERWORT, Utricularia gibba
(Utricularia biflora, fibrosa, and pumila)

Fresh water; California; and Minnesota to Nova Scotia,
Texas, and Florida.
Foliage is dense or sparse; is mixed with bladders,
or foliage and bladders are on separate branches. Flowers
are yellow.

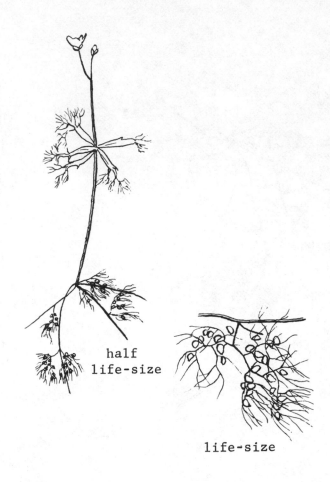

half
life-size

life-size

LITTLE FLOATING BLADDERWORT, Utricularia radiata
(Utricularia inflata var. minor)

Fresh water; Indiana to Nova Scotia, Texas, and
Florida.
    Most of the plant is under water; but its flowers
stand above a whorl of swollen, oblong, floating
leaves which have fine-forked ends. Flowers are yellow.
    Resembles Big Floating Bladderwort (page 49); but
usually is smaller, and its floats have nearly parallel
sides which pinch in near their base. Underwater
foliage resembles that of Common Bladderwort (page 45);
but it usually has more-zigzag forking and smaller
bladders.

BIG FLOATING BLADDERWORT,
Utricularia inflata

Fresh water; New
Jersey to Texas.
   Most of the plant is
under water, but its
flowers stand above a
whorl of swollen, wedge-
shaped floating leaves
which have fine-forked
ends. Flowers are
yellow.
   Resembles Little
Floating Bladderwort
(page 48); but usually
is larger, and its floats
taper all the way from
the middle to the base.
Underwater foliage re-
sembles that of Common
Bladderwort (page 45);
but it usually has more-
zigzag forking.

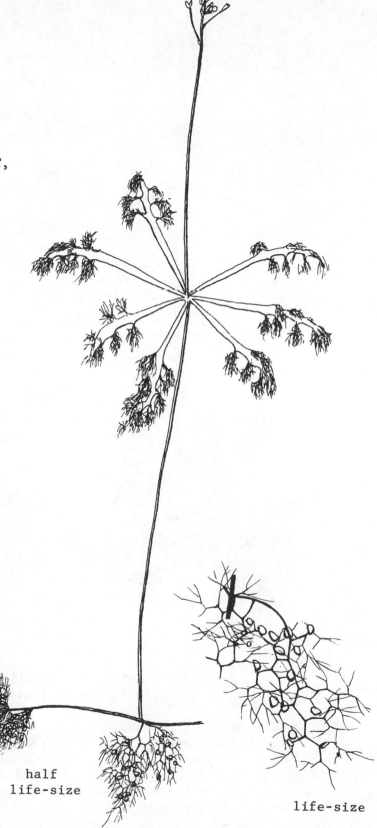

half
life-size

life-size

49

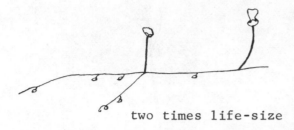

two times life-size

DWARF BLADDERWORT, Utricularia olivacea (Biovularia olivacea)

A tiny plant with whitish flowers which has been found at one locality each in New Jersey, North Carolina, South Carolina, Georgia, and Florida.

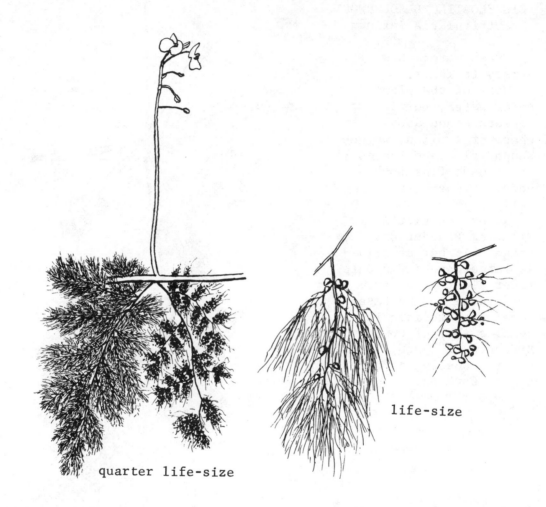

quarter life-size

life-size

GIANT BLADDERWORT, Utricularia foliosa (Utricularia floridana)

Fresh water; Louisiana to Georgia and Florida.
From a few feet to twenty feet long. Has flattish stems with two kinds of branches. One kind is a mass of threadlike green leaflets with a few interspersed bladders. The other is a mass of colorless to blackish bladders with a few interspersed leaflets. Flowers are yellow.

Group 5. PLANTS WITH CLUSTERED BRANCHES OR FINE-FORKED, BLADDERLESS, USUALLY LIMP LEAVES ON FLEXIBLE UNDERWATER STEMS; STEM TIPS SOMETIMES STICKING OUT OF WATER grow in fresh inland water and in fresh to brackish coastal water. The stems vary from upright to horizontal and from a few inches long to several feet; and they are usually branched. The underwater leaves usually collapse when taken out of water. Some kinds produce small floating or out-of-water leaves and have white, yellow, or purplish flowers at the surface of the water or a little above it.

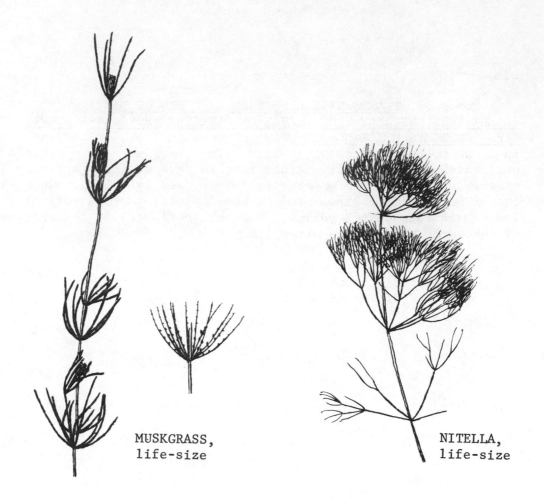

MUSKGRASS,
life-size

NITELLA,
life-size

MUSKGRASSES, Chara; NITELLAS, Nitella; TOLYPELLAS, Tolypella

Fresh to brackish water, inland and coastal; Alaska to
Greenland, California, and Florida.

Identifying these algae, which mingle with flowering plants
and resemble some of them, requires a microscope and Richard D.
Wood and Kozo Imahori's "A Revision of the Characeae" (1964-65).
These two volumes include pictures and descriptions of all of the
kinds of Characeae known from Canada and the United States: eight
Muskgrasses, twelve Nitellas, and two Tolypellas.

The different kinds vary from larger than those pictured here
to much smaller, and from more branched to less branched.

Muskgrasses usually have short, even-length branches clustered
at each joint; and these usually have clusters of much-shorter
branchlets. Usually the plants have a skunky odor; often they are
coated with lime; and sometimes they are prickly-looking.

Nitellas have short, even-length branches clustered at each
joint; and these branches often end in bushy clusters of branchlets.
The plants seldom have a skunky odor or a coating of lime.

Tolypellas (not pictured) have short branches of different
lengths clustered at each joint; therefore they look ragged.

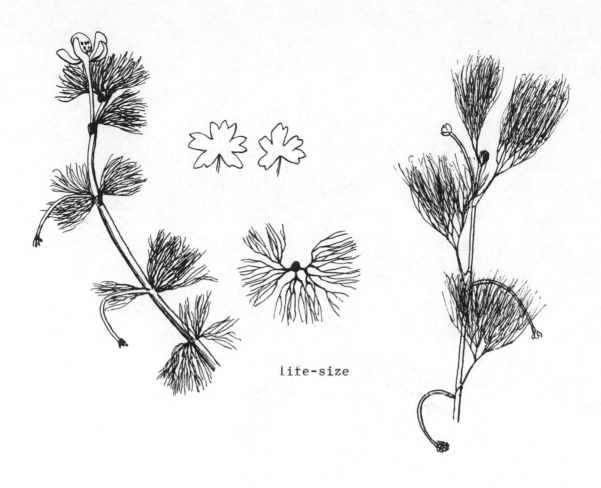

life-size

WHITE WATER BUTTERCUP, Ranunculus aquatilis
(Ranunculus longirostris, subrigidus, and trichophyllus;
Batrachium flaccidum and trichophyllum)

Fresh water, often in slow streams; Alaska to Greenland,
California, and Alabama (but rare in the southeastern states).
   Stems usually just under water. Leaves firm to limp, stalkless to long-stalked; a single stalkless leaf sometimes looking
like a cluster of several leaves. Sometimes stems have a few
floating leaves. In summer, 5-petaled flowers often whiten a
patch of water. Their stalks soon curve back into the water
and are tipped with little balls of usually a dozen or more
seeds. During low water in summer, patches of stems sometimes
grow on mud.
   Resembles Lobb Buttercup (page 113), which has mainly
floating leaves, fewer seeds in a ball, and grows only from
British Columbia to California.

53

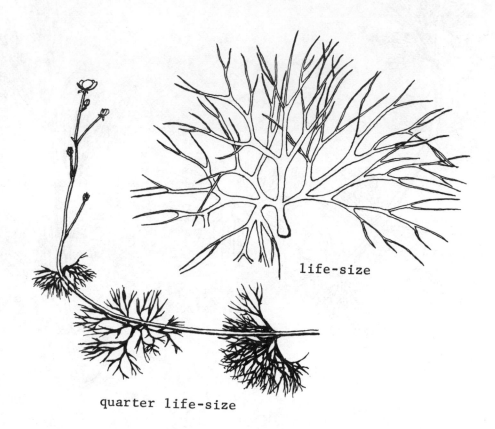

life-size

quarter life-size

YELLOW WATER BUTTERCUP, Ranunculus flabellaris
(Ranunculus delphinifolius and gmelini)

Fresh water; Alaska to Newfoundland, California, Louisiana, and North Carolina (but rare
in the southeastern states).
Stems usually just under water. Sometimes
stems have firmer, less-divided floating leaves
or out-of-water leaves. In late spring and
summer, loose clusters of 5-petaled yellow
flowers stand a little above water.

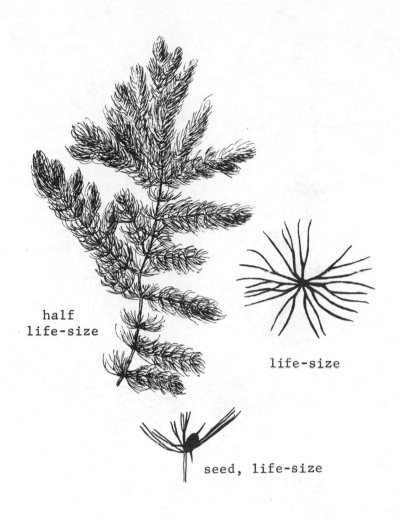

half
life-size

life-size

seed, life-size

COONTAIL, Ceratophyllum demersum
(Ceratophyllum echinatum and submersum)

Fresh water, inland and coastal; Northwest Territories to Nova Scotia, California, and Florida.
Stems entirely under water; usually much-branched,
and sometimes stiff with a coating of lime. At each
joint is a whorl of leaves. Leaflets vary in length,
width, firmness, amount of forking, and prominence of
teeth. Flowers and seeds, at base of leaves, are
usually hard to find. The commonest form of seed is
pictured. Other forms have as many as a dozen spines.

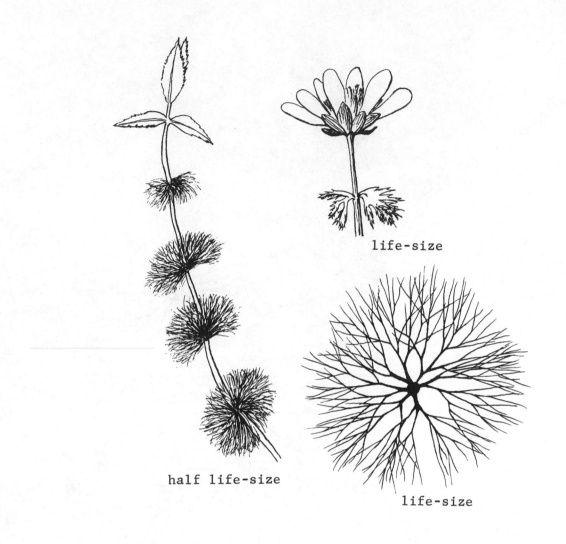

life-size

half life-size

life-size

WATER-MARIGOLD, Bidens beckii
(Megalodonta beckii)

    Fresh water; Washington and Oregon; and Saskatchewan
to Nova Scotia, Missouri, and New Jersey.
    The stalkless leaves, in pairs at each joint, look like
a cluster of several leaves. Stem tips with two or
three pairs of less-divided or merely toothed leaves
and a yellow flower head reach a little out of water.

56

LAKE CRESS,
Armoracia aquatica
(Neobeckia aquatica)

Fresh water;
Minnesota to Quebec,
Louisiana, and Flor-
ida (but rare south
of Missouri and New
York).
Stems which grow
under water have
fine-forked leaves,
the leaflets of
which are uneven-
ended. Stems or
stem tips which grow
out of water have
leaves which vary
from fine-forked to
undivided. Some-
times these out-of-
water stems have
loose clusters of
white flowers.

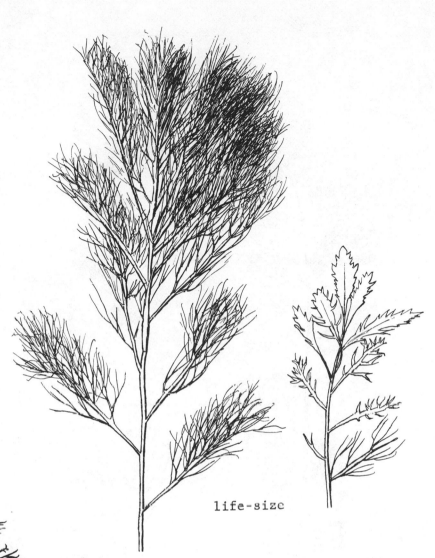

life-size

RIVERWEED on stone,
life-size

RIVERWEED,
Podostemum ceratophyllum
(Podostemon abrotanoides
and ceratophyllum)

Stony-bottom streams,
Quebec to New Brunswick,
Texas, and Georgia.
Tough stems grow in a
dull-green tangle. Their
bases cling to stones
instead of rooting among
them.

57

life-size

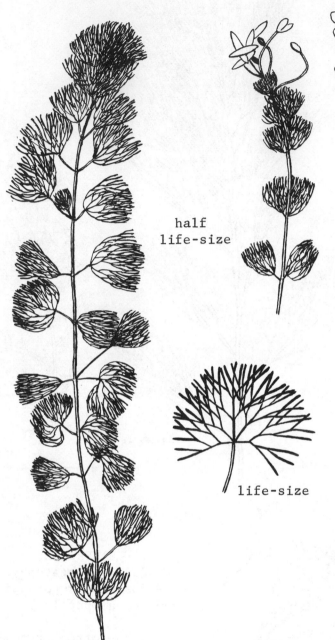

half
life-size

life-size

FANWORT,
Cabomba caroliniana

Fresh water; Michigan to New Hampshire, Texas, and Florida.
Leaves are on short or long stalks which are in pairs at each joint. Unlike most other underwater plants, the forked leaflets are a little wider at the tip than the base. Six-parted white or lavender flowers and small, narrow floating leaves are at the tip of stems which reach the surface of the water.

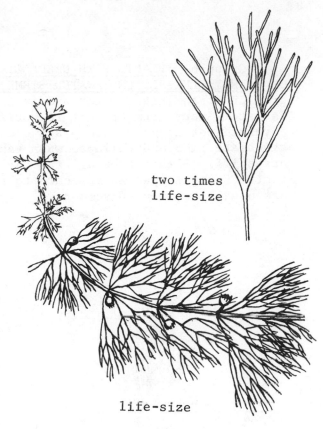

two times
life-size

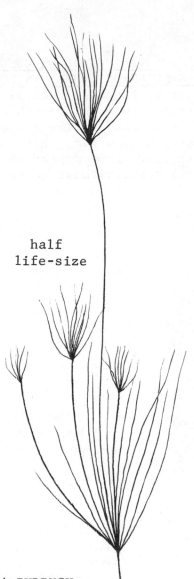

half
life-size

life-size

LIMNOPHILAS, Limnophila

Limnophila indica and Limnophila sessiliflora, natives of
southeastern Asia, are grown in
North America as aquarium
plants and have run wild in
fresh water in Texas, Louisiana, and Florida.
Out-of-water foliage looks
a little like that of Variable
Watermilfoil (page 35); but
among the leaves are purplish
flowers which produce stalkless
or short-stalked pods filled
with tiny seeds. Underwater
foliage looks a little like
that of Fanwort (page 58); but
the leaves are in clusters instead of twos; and the leaflets
are not wider at the tip than
the base.

ALGA BULRUSH,
Scirpus confervoides
(Websteria submersa)

Fresh water;
Virginia to Florida.
Hairlike stems,
as much as three
feet long, grow in
a tangle just under
water. Branches are
sometimes tipped
with a small,
spikerush-like
flower head.

Group 6. <u>PLANTS WITH NEEDLELIKE TO OVAL PAIRED OR BUNCHED LEAVES</u>
<u>ON MAINLY FLEXIBLE UNDERWATER STEMS; SOME KINDS SOMETIMES OUT OF WATER</u>
grow in fresh inland water and in fresh to brackish coastal water.
The stems vary from upright to horizontal and from an inch high to
several feet long; and they are usually branched. The leaves of some
kinds are limp and collapse when taken out of water; those of others
are stiff. Plants grow all the way to shore from depths of several
feet. Several species are hard to tell apart without seeds; but seeds
are usually common in summer.

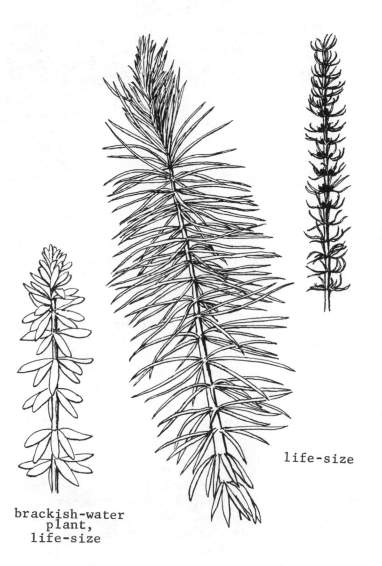

MARESTAIL,
Hippuris vulgaris
(Hippuris tetraphylla)

Fresh inland water
and brackish coastal
water; Alaska to Green-
land, California, New
Mexico, Iowa, and New
York.
Usually upright and
at least partly out of
water. Flowers and
seeds are at base of
leaves.

life-size

brackish-water
plant,
life-size

60

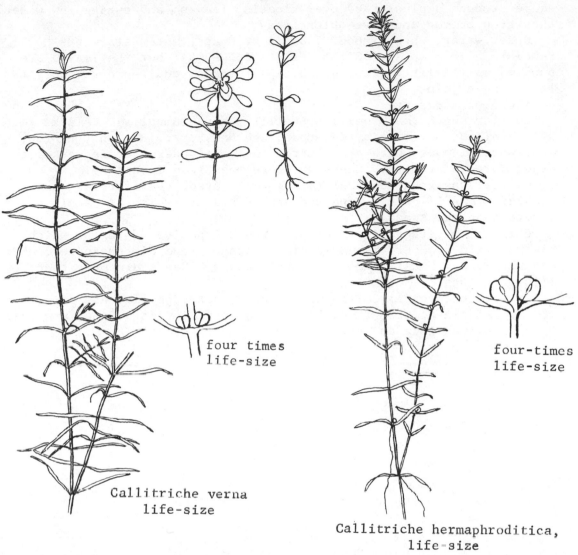

four times
life-size

Callitriche verna
life-size

four-times
life-size

Callitriche hermaphroditica,
life-size

WATER-STARWORTS, Callitriche

Fresh water, inland and rarely coastal, often in partly-shaded
streams; Alaska to Greenland, California, and Florida.

Four kinds resemble each other so much that they can be told apart
only by looking at them with a hand lens or microscope when they have
seeds. These are partly-joined to each other in fours at the base of
leaves. Under water, each of these plants has narrow leaves. All
except Callitriche hermaphroditica also often reach the surface and

there produce a cluster of oval floating leaves; and during low water they grow on mud and have oblong leaves.

Under water, when without flowers or seeds, Water-starworts resemble slim plants of Common Elodea (page 66); but the leaves are bunched only a little toward the tip of stems, and there are only two leaves at a joint.

The four kinds are:

Callitriche hermaphroditica (Callitriche autumnalis). Alaska to Newfoundland, California, Colorado, and New York. Has only narrow, underwater leaves which are shorter than the underwater leaves of the other Water-starworts. Seeds are more than 1/16 inch long.

Callitriche longipedunculata. Not pictured. California. Seeds are less than 1/16 inch long and are on a stalk which is usually longer than the seeds.

Callitriche stagnalis. Not pictured. A native of Europe which has run wild from British Columbia to Oregon; and Wisconsin to Quebec and Maryland. Usually has some oval leaves. Seeds are more than 1/16 inch long.

Callitriche verna (Callitriche anceps, heterophylla, and palustris). Alaska to Greenland, California, and Florida. Seeds are less than 1/16 inch long and have little or no stalk.

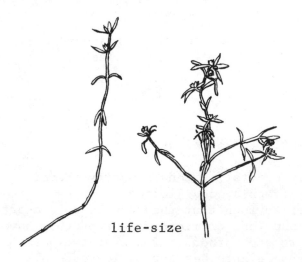

life-size

TILLAEA, Tillaea aquatica
(Tillaeastrum aquaticum)

Fresh inland water; Alaska to Northwest Territories, California, and Louisiana. And fresh to slightly brackish coastal water; Quebec to Newfoundland and Maryland; and Alabama.

Under water or partly out of water; often under water at high tide. Tiny greenish-white flowers are on very short stalks at base of leaves.

HORNED-PONDWEED
Zannichellia palustris

Fresh and alkali inland water and fresh and brackish coastal water; Alaska to Newfoundland, California, and Florida.

From spring to fall a person can usually find the seeds, which are unlike those of any other plant.

Without seeds, Horned-pondweed resembles Slender (page 75), Leafy (page 77), Snailseed (page 78), and Vasey (page 80) Pondweeds; but it has leaves in pairs at all the joints of a stem.

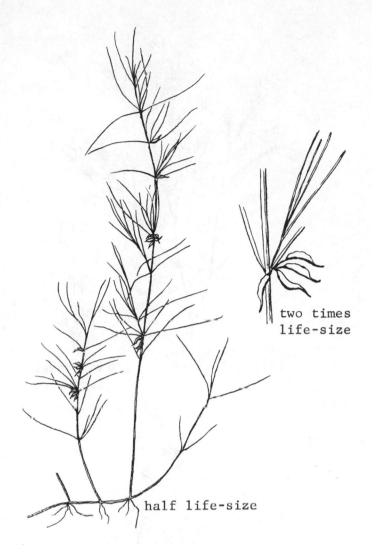

two times
life-size

half life-size

WATERWORTS, Elatine

Fresh water, inland and coastal; Northwest Territories to Newfoundland, California, and Georgia.

Three kinds resemble each other so much that they can be told apart only by using a microscope to look at the shape of seeds and the shape of their surface markings. The seeds are in pinhead-sized, transparent-walled pods at the base of leaves.

The three kinds are:

Elatine californica. Washington to Montana, California, and Arizona.

Elatine minima. Minnesota to Newfoundland and Virginia

Elatine triandra (Elatine ambigua, americana, brachysperma, chilensis, gracilis, heterandra, obovata, and rubella). Northwest Territories to New Brunswick, California, and Georgia.

life-size

Najas flexilis,
half life-size

two times
life-size

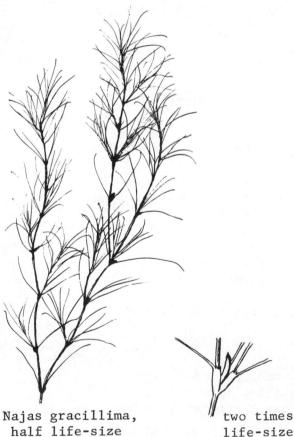

Najas gracillima,
half life-size

two times
life-size

NAIADS, Najas
(except SPINY NAIAD, page 67)

Fresh inland water and
fresh to slightly brackish
coastal water; British Columbia to Newfoundland, California, and Florida.

Six kinds resemble each
other so much that they can
be told apart only by using a
hand lens or microscope to
look at the toothing of leaf
edges, the shape and toothing
of leaf bases, and the markings on seeds. Tops of plants
are often almost out of sight
under water. Plants vary in
size from tufts an inch high
on sandy bottom to much-
branched plants two or three
feet high on silty bottom.

The six kinds are:

Najas conferta. Not pic-
tured. Southwestern Georgia
and western Florida. Leaves
usually curve out from the
stem, and their marginal teeth
are visible to the naked eye.
Resembles minor (page 65); but
the seeds are not ribbed
lengthwise.

Najas flexilis. British
Columbia to Newfoundland, California, Missouri, and Virginia.
Leaves usually curve out from
the stem. Unlike the other
kinds, its seeds are shiny
under the dull, easily-rubbed-
off skin.

Najas gracillima. Minne-
sota to Maine, Missouri, and
North Carolina. Threadlike
leaves usually curve out from
the stem. Resembles flexilis;
but usually has slenderer

leaves and has wide-
topped leaf bases and
dull seeds.

Najas graminea.
Not pictured. A
native of the Old
World which has run
wild in California
ricefields. Very
bushy with leaves
which usually curve
out from the stem.
Resembles flexilis
(page 64); but has
dull seeds.

Najas guadalupen-
sis (Najas muenscheri
and olivacea). Oregon
to Quebec, California,
and Florida. Leaves
are shorter than in
the other kinds, usu-
ally do not curve out-
ward, and are not much
bunched. When without
seeds, guadalupensis
resembles underwater
forms of Water-star-
wort (page 61); but
the leaves have
sheathing bases.

Najas minor.
Illinois to Vermont,
Alabama, and Florida.
A native of Eurasia
which in the last
forty years has be-
come common in the
tidal Hudson River
and in artificial
lakes. Leaves usually
curve outward, and
their marginal teeth
are visible to the
naked eye. Unlike
the other kinds, its
seeds are ribbed
lengthwise.

two times
life-size

Najas guadalupensis,
half life-size

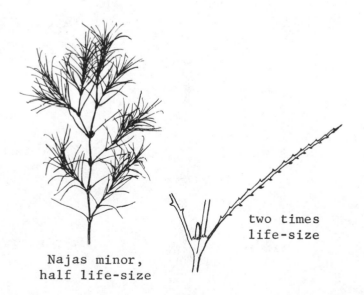

two times
life-size

Najas minor,
half life-size

COMMON ELODEA, Elodea canadensis
(Elodea nuttallii; Philotria
canadensis and linearis)

Fresh to slightly alkali inland
water and fresh to slightly brackish
coastal water; British Columbia to
Quebec, California, and Florida.

Leaves vary greatly in width,
size, and bunching; therefore plants
are often slimmer or stouter than
as pictured. Sometimes there are
slim seed pods at the base of leaves.

Big plants resemble small plants
of South American Elodea (page 68);
but toward the tip of stems the
leaves of Common are in twos or
threes at a joint, those of South
American are in fours or fives.
Plants with narrow, limp leaves resemble underwater forms of Water-
starworts (page 61); but Elodea
leaves are bunched toward the tip of
stems and usually are in threes at
a joint. Resembles large plants of
Micranthemum (page 70); but Elodea
leaves are usually bunched at the
end of branches.

life-size

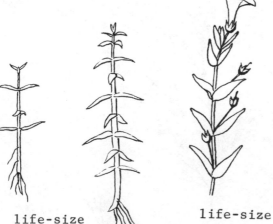

life-size   life-size

GOLDENPERT, Gratiola aurea

Fresh water; Wisconsin to
Newfoundland, Alabama, and
Florida (but only near the
coast in the southeastern
states).

Sometimes grows in several
feet of water, where it is
an inch or two high and has
sharp-tipped leaves and no
flowers. Usually grows out
of water or partly out; then
is bigger and has blunt-
tipped leaves and yellow
flowers.

66

MARSH-PURSLANE,
Ludwigia palustris
(Ludwigia natans; Isnardia
intermedia, palustris, and
repens)

Fresh water; British
Columbia to Nova Scotia,
California, and Florida.
Usually sprawls on wet
ground or partly under
water; but sometimes in
clear springs and spring-
fed streams it has about
the same appearance as
when it grows out of
water.

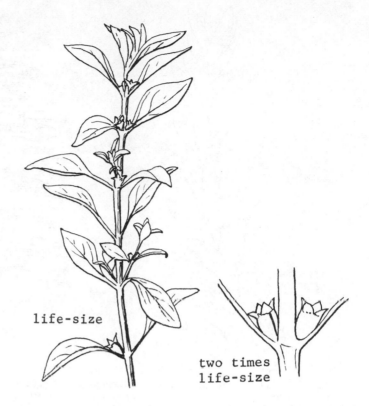

life-size

two times
life-size

SPINY NAIAD, Najas marina
(Najas gracilis)

Fresh, brackish, and
alkali inland water, and
rarely brackish coastal
water; California to Utah
and Arizona; North Dakota
to New York; southern
Texas; and Florida.
Varies greatly in
coarseness; but teeth are
conspicuous on the leaves
of even the smallest,
slimmest plants.

two times
life-size

half life-size

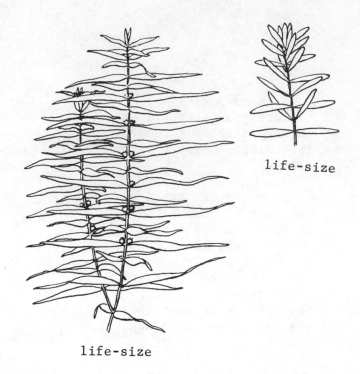

life-size

life-size

life-size

WATER-PURSLANE, Peplis diandra
(Didiplis diandra)

Fresh water; Wisconsin to Virginia,
Texas, and Florida.
Under water or out of water. Underwater leaves are limp and ribbonlike.
Out-of-water leaves are stiffer and
shorter. Often has ball-like seed pods,
less than 1/8 inch across, at the base
of leaves.

SOUTH AMERICAN ELODEA, Elodea densa
(Philotria densa)

This common aquarium plant has run wild in fresh
inland and rarely coastal water from Oregon to Massachusetts, California, and Florida.
Usually in a branched tangle just under water.
Sometimes the 3-petaled flowers whiten a patch of
surface.
Small plants resemble big plants of Common Elodea
(page 66); but toward the tip of stems the leaves of
South American are in fours or fives at a joint,
those of Common are in twos and threes.

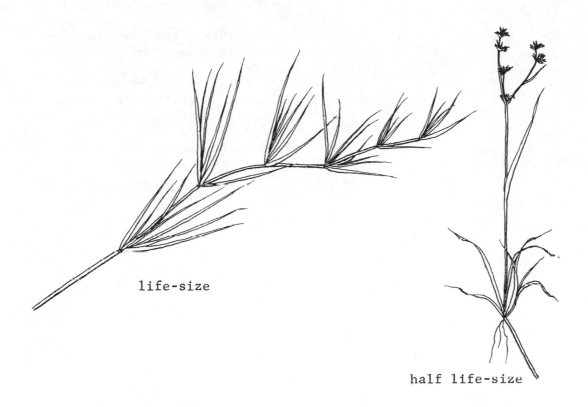

life-size

half life-size

CREEPING RUSH, Juncus repens

    Fresh water; Oklahoma to Delaware, Texas, and
Florida.
    In mats under water, floating, or out of water.
Stems are several times as wide as thick. Leaves
and clusters of leaves are flat.

MICRANTHEMUM, Micranthemum micranthemoides
(Hemianthus glomeratus)

Fresh coastal water from New York to Virginia; and fresh inland and coastal water in Florida.

Grows under water or partly out of water; often under water at high tide. Varies from smaller than pictured to larger and more branched.

Large plants resemble Common Elodea (page 66); but Micranthemum leaves are usually not bunched at the end of branches.

life-size

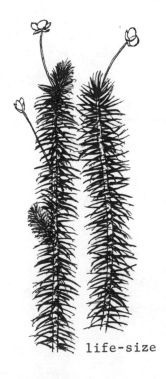

MAYACA, Mayaca fluviatilis
(Mayaca aubletii)

Fresh water; North Carolina to Texas.

Under water or partly out of water. Has 3-petaled pink flowers.

When not in bloom, resembles Bog Clubmoss.

life-size

70

Group 7. <u>PLANTS WITH THREADLIKE TO RIBBONLIKE LEAVES SCATTERED</u>
<u>SINGLY ON FLEXIBLE UNDERWATER STEMS, BUT OFTEN PAIRED OR BUNCHED</u>
<u>TOWARD THE STEM TIPS; A FEW KINDS ALSO WITH OBLONG TO OVAL FLOATING</u>
<u>LEAVES</u> grow in fresh inland water and in fresh to salt coastal water.
The stems vary from upright to horizontal and from a few inches long
to several feet; and usually they reach almost to the surface of the
water, or even trail just beneath or on it. The underwater leaves
collapse or partly collapse when taken out of water. In summer,
Pondweeds produce small greenish or brownish flowers which are usually
close together in oblong or ball-like spikes. In bloom, the upper
spikes often stand above water; but when the seeds are ripe, the spikes
are usually lying in water. Water-stargrass has scattered yellow
flowers and slim seed pods. Widgeongrass has pondweed-like flowers
which ripen a small cluster of long-stalked seeds.

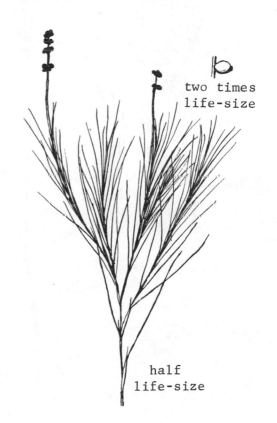

two times
life-size

THREADLEAF PONDWEED,
Potamogeton filiformis

Fresh inland water and fresh
to slightly brackish coastal water;
Alaska to Greenland, California,
New Mexico, Minnesota, and Pennsylvania.
Resembles Sago Pondweed (page
72); but the stems are usually
shorter, and the smaller seeds
(a little less than 1/8 inch
long) have a flattish, wart-
like tip. Resembles Bigsheath
Pondweed (page 74); but is
smaller, all the leaves have
narrow-sheathed bases, and the
seed heads usually have only 3
or 4 clusters of seeds.

half
life-size

71

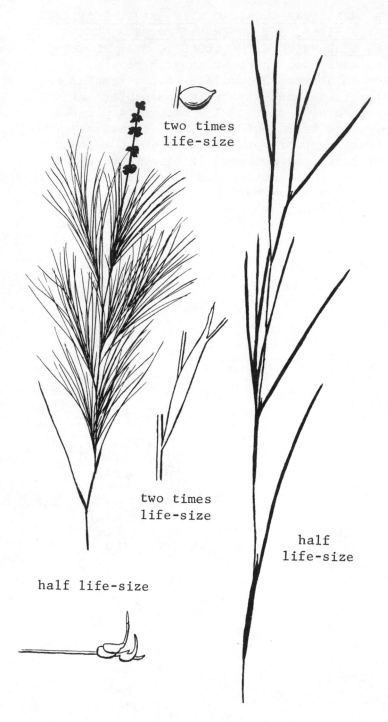

two times
life-size

half life-size

two times
life-size

half
life-size

SAGO PONDWEED,
Potamogeton pectinatus

Fresh and alkali
inland water and fresh
to brackish coastal
water; Alaska to Que-
bec, California, and
Florida (but rare in
the southeastern
states).

Resembles Thread-
leaf Pondweed (page
71); but the stems
are usually longer,
and the larger seeds
(1/8 inch long or
more) have a pointed
tip. Resembles Big-
sheath Pondweed (page
74); but all the
leaves have narrow-
sheathed bases, and
the seeds have a
pointed tip. When
not in bloom or seed,
resembles non-seeding
Widgeongrass (page
73); but the leaves
are usually in
bushier clusters, the
sheathing base of the
leaves has a tapering,
flimsy tip, and the
rootstocks are long
and straight and
often have tubers.

two times
life-size

half life-size

WIDGEONGRASS, Ruppia maritima
(Ruppia occidentalis)

Salt to fresh coastal water and alkali to fresh
inland water; Alaska to Newfoundland, California,
and Florida (but very rare inland in the eastern
half of the continent).

When not in seed, resembles non-seeding Sago
Pondweed (page 72); but the leaves are usually
in less-bushy clusters, the sheathing base of the
leaves has a rounded, firm tip, and the rootstocks are short and zigzag and have no tubers.

half life-size

BIGSHEATH PONDWEED,
Potamogeton vaginatus

   Fresh water;
Alaska to Quebec,
Oregon, Colorado, and
New York.
   Resembles Sago
Pondweed (page 72);
but the sheathing
base of the main
leaves is two or more
times as wide as the
stem, and the seeds
have a flattish wart-
like tip. Resembles
Threadleaf Pondweed
(page 71); but is
bigger, the sheathing
base of the main
leaves is two or
more times as wide
as the stem, and the
heads usually have
6-10 clusters of
seeds.

SLENDER PONDWEED,
Potamogeton pusillus
(Potamogeton berchtoldi,
gemmiparus, and lateralis)

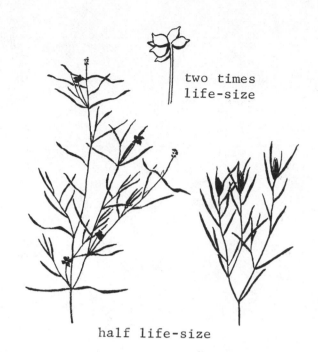

two times
life-size

half life-size

Fresh and alkali inland
water and fresh and slightly
brackish coastal water;
Alaska to Greenland, California, and Florida.
 Resembles Leafy Pondweed
(page 77); but has longer-
stalked seed heads and blunt-
backed seeds. Resembles
Fries Pondweed (below); but
has smaller seeds (a little
more than 1/16 inch long)
usually smaller leaves, and
smaller, smooth-leaved winterbuds. Resembles the underwater form of Snailseed
Pondweed (page 78); but has
longer-stalked seed heads,
convex-sided seeds, and
leaves with non-sheathing
base. Resembles the underwater form of Vasey Pondweed
(page 80); but has bigger,
fatter winterbuds.

FRIES PONDWEED,
Potamogeton friesii
(Potamogeton longiligulatus
and strictifolius)

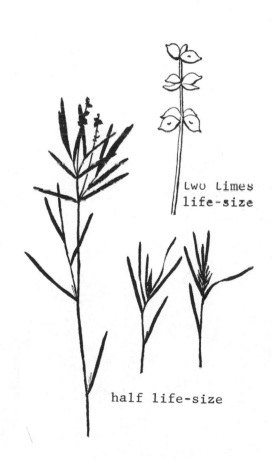

two times
life-size

half life-size

Fresh water; Northwest Territories to Newfoundland, Washington,
Utah, and Virginia.
 Resembles Slender Pondweed
(above); but has bigger seeds
(nearly 1/8 inch long), usually
bigger leaves, and bigger winterbuds with leaves corrugated at
the base with raised veins.
Resembles Bluntleaf and Leafy
Pondweeds (page 77); but has
longer-stalked, looser seed
heads and blunt-backed seeds.

FLATSTEM PONDWEED,
Potamogeton zosteriformis

    Fresh water, inland
and rarely coastal;
Alaska to Quebec, Cali-
fornia, Nebraska, and
Virginia.
    Stems several times
as wide as thick.
    When not in bloom,
resembles non-blooming
Water-stargrass (page 79);
but has leaves with
prominent midvein and
non-sheathing base.

half life-size

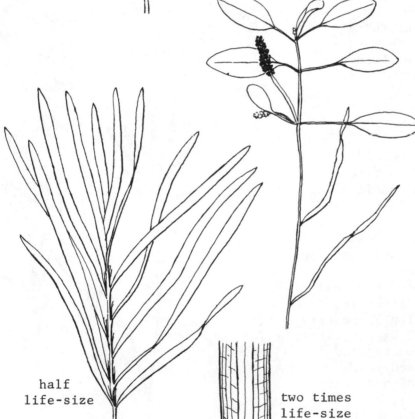

RIBBONLEAF PONDWEED,
Potamogeton epihydrus

    Fresh water,
inland, particularly
in slow streams, and
rarely coastal;
Alaska to Quebec,
California, Colo-
rado, and Georgia.
    The very limp
underwater leaves
have a light-colored
center stripe.
Usually there are
floating leaves.

half
life-size

two times
life-size

LEAFY PONDWEED,
Potamogeton foliosus
(Potamogeton curtissii, fibril-
losus, hillii, and porteri)

Fresh and alkali inland
water and fresh and slightly
brackish coastal water; Northwest Territories to Quebec,
California, and Florida.
Resembles Slender and
Fries Pondweeds (page 75);
but has shorter-stalked seed
heads, and seeds with a knife-
edge back. Resembles Bluntleaf Pondweed (below); but has
sharp-tipped, usually smaller
leaves, and ball-like clusters
of usually smaller seeds.
Resembles the underwater form
of Snailseed Pondweed (page
78); but Leafy's leaves do
not have a sheathing base, and
its seeds are not snail-like.
Resembles the underwater form
of Vasey Pondweed (page 80);
but has bigger, fatter,
winterbuds, shorter-stalked
seed heads, and seeds with a
knife-edge back.

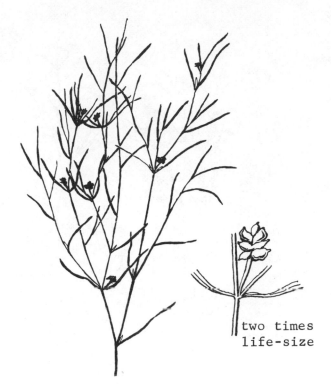

two times
life-size

half life-size

BLUNTLEAF PONDWEED,
Potamogeton obtusifolius

Fresh water, often in slow
streams; Alaska to Quebec, Wyoming,
Michigan, and New Jersey.
Resembles Leafy Pondweed (above);
but has round-tipped, usually
larger leaves, and oblong clusters
of usually larger seeds. Resembles
Fries Pondweed (page 75); but has
shorter-stalked, denser seed heads,
and larger (1/8 inch long or more),
sharp-backed seeds.

half life-size

77

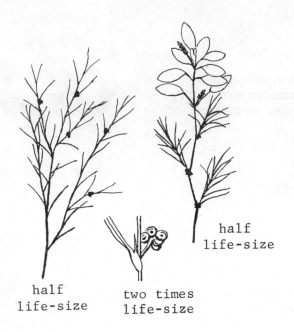

SNAILSEED PONDWEED,
Potamogeton diversifolius
(Potamogeton bicupulatus,
capillaceus, and spirillus)

Fresh water, inland and rarely coastal; Montana to Newfoundland, California, and Florida.

Usually there are floating leaves. Without them, Snailseed Pondweed resembles Slender (page 75), Leafy (page 77), Vasey (page 80), and Alga (below) Pondweeds; but its leaf bases make a sheath around the stem, and it usually has several ball-like, almost stalkless underwater seed heads, with the seeds resembling tiny, flat snails.

half
life-size

two times
life-size

half
life-size

ALGA PONDWEED,
Potamogeton confervoides

Fresh water; Wisconsin to Newfoundland and New Jersey; and North Carolina.

The bunched leaves are flimsy and hairlike.

Without seeds, it resembles the slimmest form of Snailseed Pondweed (above); but its leaves do not have a sheathing base.

half
life-size

FERN PONDWEED,
Potamogeton robbinsii

Fresh water, inland
and rarely coastal;
British Columbia to Wyo-
ming, California, and
Utah; Manitoba to Nova
Scotia, Minnesota, and
Virginia; and Alabama.
  Leaf bases make a
sheath around the stem.
Often these are whitish,
overlapping, and frayed
into short threads.
The form pictured grows
in colonies with the
tips of stems often a
foot or more under
water. A longer-stemmed,
sprawly form has a less-
fernlike look.

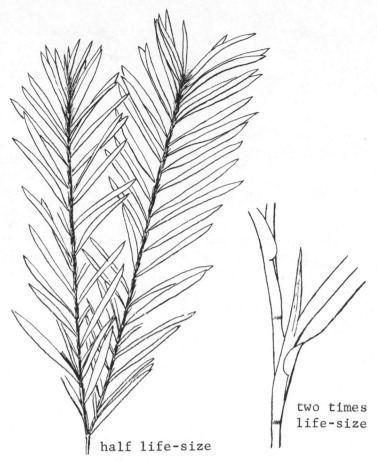

two times
life-size

half life-size

WATER-STARGRASS, Heteranthera dubia
(Zosterella dubia)

Fresh water, inland and rarely
coastal; Washington to Quebec, California, and Florida (but rare from
the Rockies west).
  Yellow flowers are followed by
slim pods with tiny seeds. Short
plants sprawling on wet mud grow
and bloom as well as longer ones do
in water.
  When not in bloom, resembles
non-blooming Flatstem Pondweed
(page 76); but has leaves without
a noticeable midvein and with a
base that makes a sheath around
the stem.

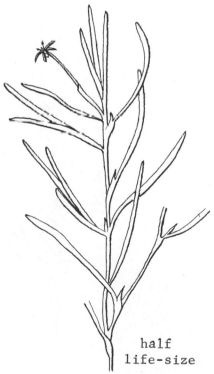

half
life-size

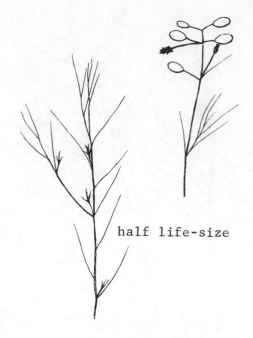

VASEY PONDWEED, Potamogeton vaseyi

Fresh water; Minnesota to New Brunswick, Iowa, and Pennsylvania.

Leaves hairlike and with long-tapered tips. Often there are tiny winterbuds on short stalks at the base of leaves. Sometimes there are floating leaves.

When without floating leaves, Vasey Pondweed resembles the slimmest form of Slender Pondweed (page 75); but it has smaller, slimmer winterbuds.

half life-size

WESTERN PONDWEED,
Potamogeton latifolius

Alkali water; Oregon to California and Texas.

The short, ribbonlike, blunt-tipped leaves have a base which makes a sheath two or more times the width of the stem. Seed heads and seeds resemble those of Sago Pondweed (page 72).

half
life-size

Group 8. <u>PLANTS WITH LANCE-SHAPED TO OVAL LEAVES SCATTERED
SINGLY ON FLEXIBLE UNDERWATER STEMS, BUT OFTEN PAIRED OR BUNCHED
TOWARD THE STEM TIPS; SOME KINDS ALSO WITH OBLONG TO OVAL FLOATING
LEAVES</u> grow in fresh inland water and in fresh to brackish coastal
water. The stems vary from upright to horizontal; frequently are
several feet long; and are usually branched. Usually they reach
almost to the surface of the water; and Red, Variable, and Bigleaf
Pondweed stems are often tipped with floating leaves. In summer,
these Pondweeds produce small greenish or brownish flowers which are
close together in oblong spikes. In bloom, the spikes often stand
above water; but when the seeds are ripe the spikes are usually
lying in water.

half life-size

RED PONDWEED, Potamogeton alpinus

    Fresh water, often in slow streams; Alaska to Greenland, Cali-
fornia, Colorado, Wisconsin, and Pennsylvania.
    Plants are usually reddish. Sometimes they have floating leaves.
    Resembles plants of Variable Pondweed (page 82) with long under-
water leaves and no floating leaves; but Red Pondweed is usually
only a little branched.

81

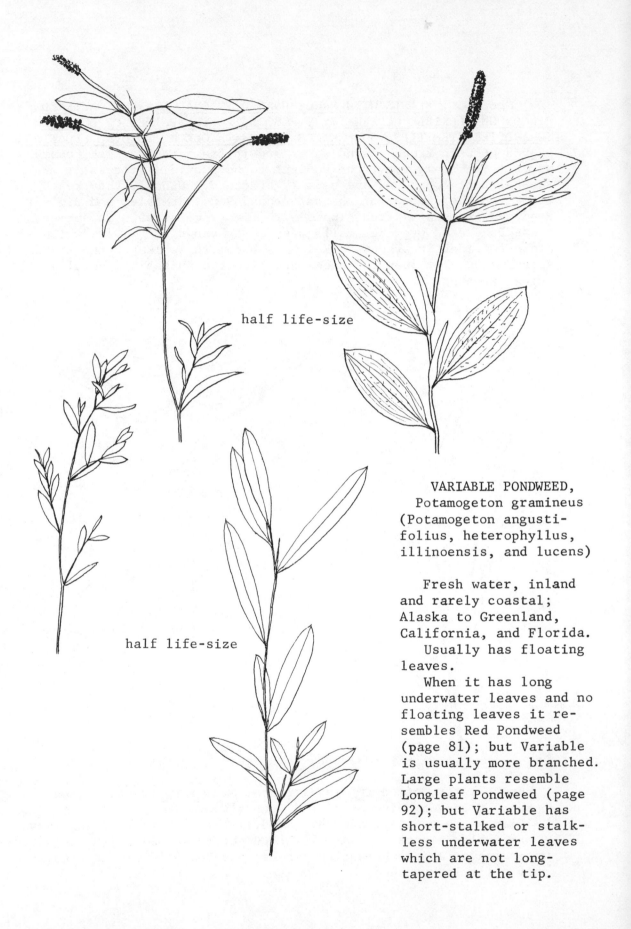

half life-size

half life-size

VARIABLE PONDWEED,
Potamogeton gramineus
(Potamogeton angusti-
folius, heterophyllus,
illinoensis, and lucens)

Fresh water, inland
and rarely coastal;
Alaska to Greenland,
California, and Florida.
    Usually has floating
leaves.
    When it has long
underwater leaves and no
floating leaves it re-
sembles Red Pondweed
(page 81); but Variable
is usually more branched.
Large plants resemble
Longleaf Pondweed (page
92); but Variable has
short-stalked or stalk-
less underwater leaves
which are not long-
tapered at the tip.

82

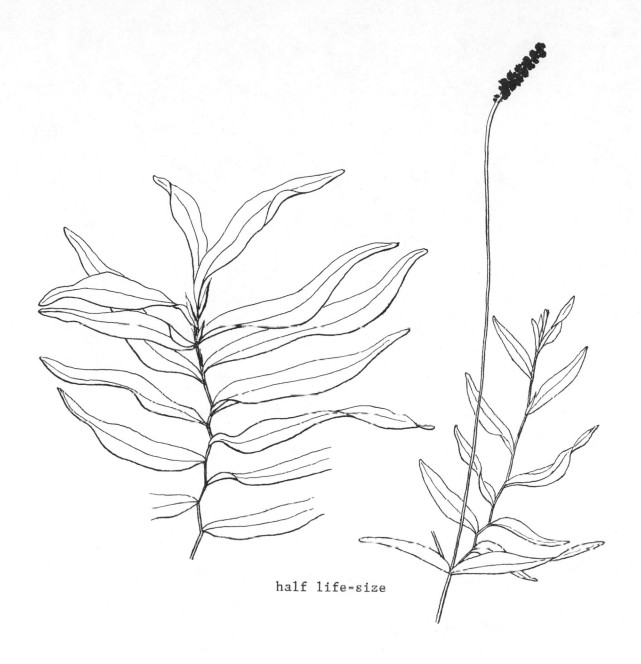

half life-size

WHITESTEM PONDWEED, Potamogeton praelongus

    Fresh water; Alaska to Newfoundland, California, Colo-
rado, and New Jersey.
    Leaves sometimes puckered.
    Resembles long-leaved plants of Redhead-grass (page 84);
but Whitestem's leaves have a hooded tip which splits a
little way back when it is flattened, the upper part of
stems is usually zigzag, the seed heads are long-stalked,
and the sharp-backed seeds are about 3/16 inch long.

half life-size

REDHEAD-GRASS, Potamogeton perfoliatus
(Potamogeton richardsonii)

Fresh inland water; Alaska to Newfoundland, California,
Arizona, Nebraska, and New Jersey. And fresh to brackish
coastal water; Newfoundland to Texas (but rare south of
North Carolina).
Leaves vary from oval and flat to lance-shaped and
puckered.
Long-leaved plants resemble Whitestem Pondweed (page 83);
but the leaves have a flat tip, the upper part of stems is
usually straight, the seed heads are short-stalked, and the
blunt-backed seeds are about 1/8 inch long.

half life size

BIGLEAF PONDWEED, Potamogeton amplifolius

Fresh water, inland and rarely coastal; British Columbia to Newfoundland, California, Oklahoma, and Georgia (but rare in the Rockies and Great Basin).
Underwater leaves are usually strongly-arched lengthwise. Usually there are floating leaves.

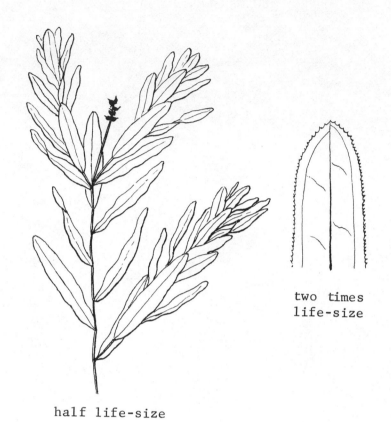

two times
life-size

half life-size

CURLY PONDWEED, Potamogeton crispus

    Fresh inland water and fresh to slightly brackish
coastal water; Alberta to Quebec, California, and
Florida. This native of the Old World has been in North
America for at least 150 years and is still spreading.
Leaves have finely-toothed, usually puckered edges.

Group 9. <u>PLANTS WITH LANCE-SHAPED TO ROUND FLOATING LEAVES</u>
<u>WHICH ARE TAPERED TO SLIGHTLY NOTCHED AT THE BASE; SOME KINDS ALSO</u>
<u>WITH THREADLIKE TO OVAL UNDERWATER LEAVES; AND SOME KINDS ALSO</u>
<u>GROWING PARTLY OUT OF WATER</u> grow in fresh inland water and in fresh
coastal water. The leaves of some kinds are on flexible, upright to
horizontal stems; others have leaves in clumps on the bottom or
coming up from rootstocks. Flowers vary from the inconspicuous ones
of Pondweeds to the showy yellowish ones of American Lotus.

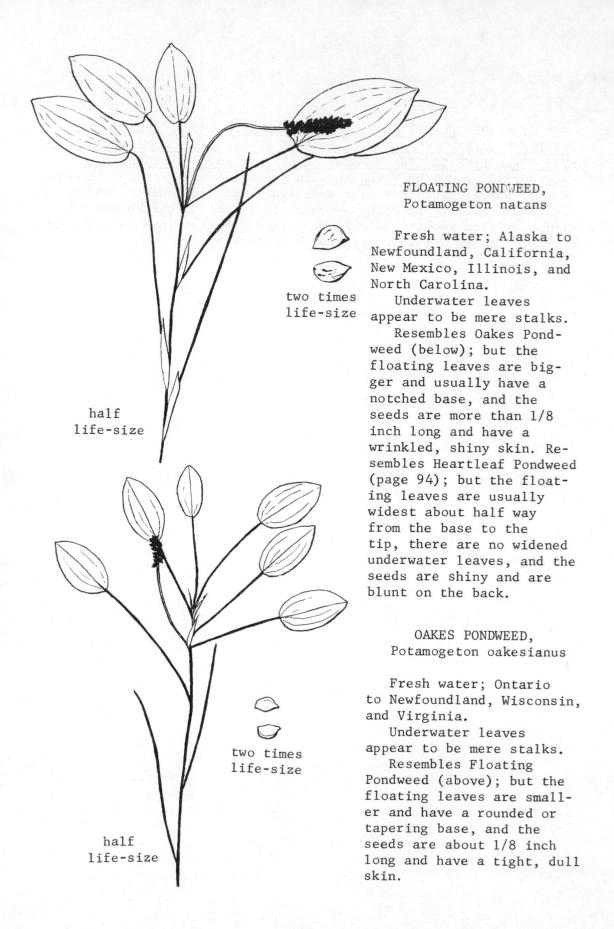

two times
life-size

half
life-size

two times
life-size

half
life-size

FLOATING PONDWEED,
Potamogeton natans

Fresh water; Alaska to
Newfoundland, California,
New Mexico, Illinois, and
North Carolina.
Underwater leaves
appear to be mere stalks.
Resembles Oakes Pond-
weed (below); but the
floating leaves are big-
ger and usually have a
notched base, and the
seeds are more than 1/8
inch long and have a
wrinkled, shiny skin. Re-
sembles Heartleaf Pondweed
(page 94); but the float-
ing leaves are usually
widest about half way
from the base to the
tip, there are no widened
underwater leaves, and the
seeds are shiny and are
blunt on the back.

OAKES PONDWEED,
Potamogeton oakesianus

Fresh water; Ontario
to Newfoundland, Wisconsin,
and Virginia.
Underwater leaves
appear to be mere stalks.
Resembles Floating
Pondweed (above); but the
floating leaves are smaller and have a rounded or
tapering base, and the
seeds are about 1/8 inch
long and have a tight, dull
skin.

half life-size

WATER SMARTWEED, Polygonum amphibium
(Polygonum natans)

   Fresh water; Alaska to Quebec, California, Illinois,
and New Jersey.
   Heads of pink flowers stand above water. An upright
form grows in wet soil or reaches high above shallow water.
   Resembles Marsh Smartweed (page 90); but the shorter
clusters of flowers are on hairless stalks, and the leaves
are smaller and narrower.

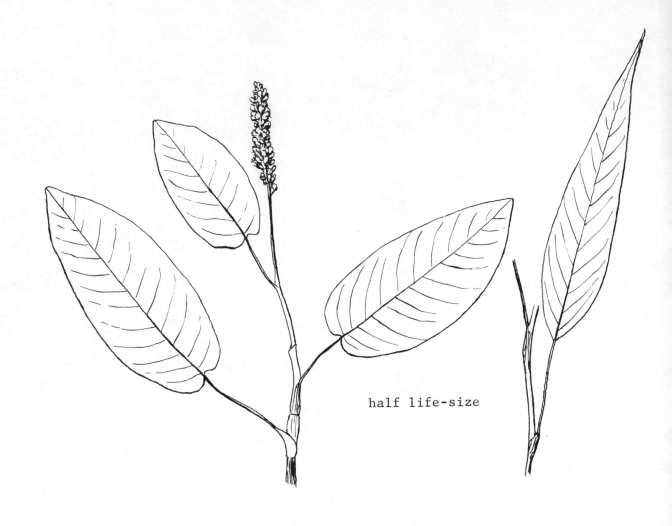

half life-size

MARSH SMARTWEED, Polygonum coccineum
(Persicaria muhlenbergii)

Fresh water; British Columbia to Quebec, California,
Texas, and South Carolina.
Heads of pink flowers stand above water. A commoner,
upright form grows in wet soil or reaches high above shallow
water.
Resembles Water Smartweed (page 89); but the longer
clusters of flowers are on fine-hairy stalks, and the
leaves are bigger and wider.

90

BOG PONDWEED,
Potamogeton oblongus

Fresh water;
Newfoundland to Nova
Scotia.
Seeds are red,
nearly round in side
view, and a little
more than 1/16 inch
long.

half
life-size

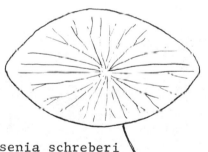

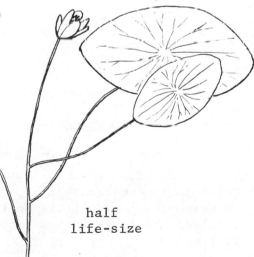

WATERSHIELD, Brasenia schreberi

Fresh water; Brisish Columbia to Idaho and California;
and Minnesota to Quebec, Texas,
and Florida.
The stalk is attached to the
middle of a leaf. Leaf buds,
flower buds, and underside of
leaves are covered with
slippery jelly. Each dull-red
flower produces a cluster of
pods which contain one or two
seeds apiece.

half
life-size

half life-size

LONGLEAF PONDWEED, Potamogeton nodosus
(Potamogeton fluitans)

Fresh, often flowing water, inland and rarely coastal; British
Columbia to New Brunswick, California, and Florida.
Resembles large plants of Variable Pondweed (page 82); but
Longleaf has long-stalked underwater leaves which are long-tapered
at the tip.

92

BROADLEAF WATERPLANTAIN,
Alisma plantago-aquatica
(Alisma subcordatum and
triviale)

Fresh water; British
Columbia to Nova Scotia,
California, and Florida.
Clustered early
leaves often float.
Later leaves stand above
water or mud around one
or more loose flower
heads.
Early leaves resemble
those of Upright Burhead
(page 96); but mature
plants have sharp-tipped
leaves and little cir-
cles of flattish, round-
tipped seeds. Out-of-
water plants resemble
Narrowleaf Waterplantain
(page 9); but the leaves
usually have a blunt or
notched base, and the
clusters of flowers are
longer than the leaves.

half life-size

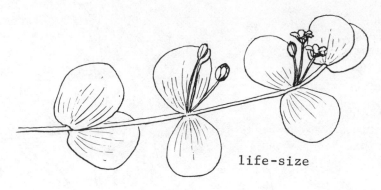

ROUNDLEAF BACOPA,
Bacopa rotundifolia
(Bacopa eisenii and
nobsiana; Macuillamia
rotundifolia)

Fresh water; British
Columbia to Manitoba,
California, Louisiana,
and North Carolina.
Flowers are white.

life-size

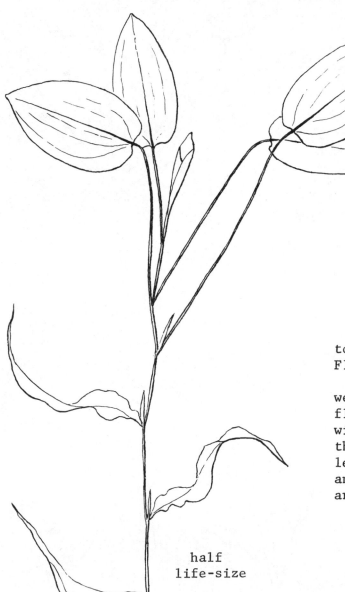

HEARTLEAF PONDWEED,
Potamogeton pulcher

Fresh water; Minnesota
to Nova Scotia, Texas, and
Florida.
Resembles Floating Pond-
weed (page 88); but the
floating leaves are usually
widest nearer the base than
the tip, the underwater
leaves are lance-shaped,
and the seeds are dull and
are sharp-backed.

half
life-size

94

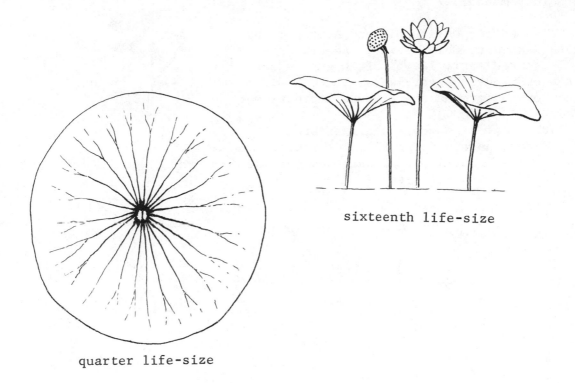

sixteenth life-size

quarter life-size

AMERICAN LOTUS, Nelumbo lutea

Fresh water, inland and rarely coastal; Minnesota to
Massachusetts, Texas, and Florida.

Grayish-green leaves which are as much as 2 feet across
float or stand above water. When standing, they often
look like partly-wrongside-out umbrellas. The pale-yellow
fragrant flowers are as much as 10 inches across. The
acornlike seeds are in individual pits in a flat-topped
receptacle. When not quite ripe, they taste like chestnuts.

UPRIGHT BURHEAD, Echinodorus berteroi
(Echinodorus cordifolius in Mason's and
Small's manuals; Echinodorus rostratus in
Fernald's manual)

   Fresh water; California and Arizona; and
South Dakota to Ohio, Texas, and Arkansas.
   Clustered early leaves often grow under
water or float. Later leaves stand above
water or mud around one or more loose flower
heads.
   Early leaves resemble those of Broadleaf Waterplantain (page 93); but mature
plants have blunt-tipped leaves and burlike
balls of sharp-pointed seeds.

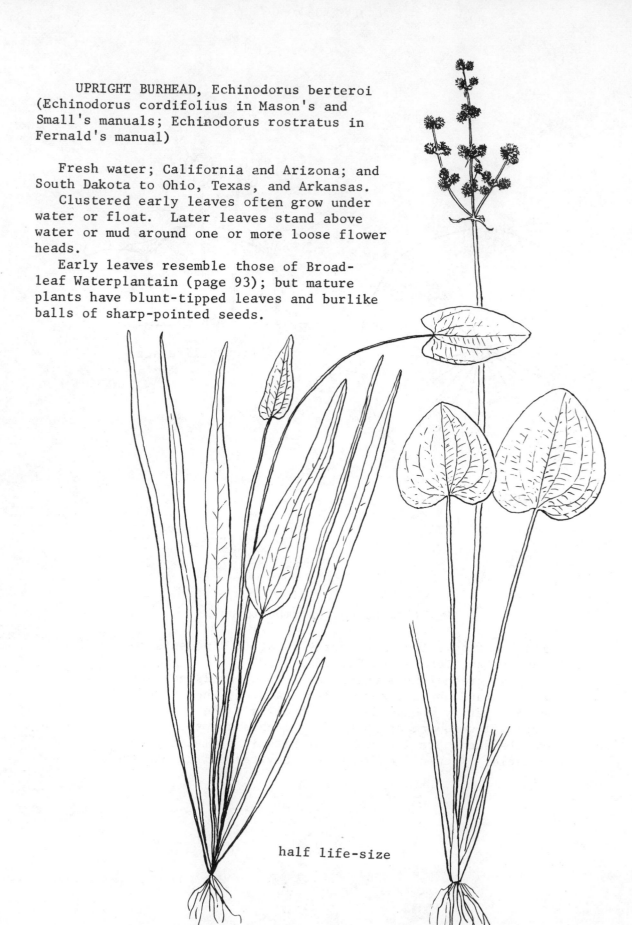

half life-size

96

LONGLEAF MUDPLANTAIN,
Heteranthera limosa

Fresh water; Colorado
to Minnesota, Arizona,
Louisiana, and Kentucky.
Leaves are under water,
floating, or out of water.
Flowers are blue or white.

half
life-size

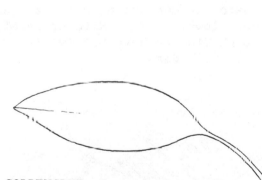

GOLDENCLUB, Orontium aquaticum

Fresh water, inland and
coastal; Iowa to Massachusetts,
Louisiana, and Florida.
Leaves float or grow out
of water. Their upperside has
a satiny sheen; underside is
whitish and has many lengthwise-
running veins. Flower spike is
yellow; the thick upper part of
its stalk is white.

half
life-size

97

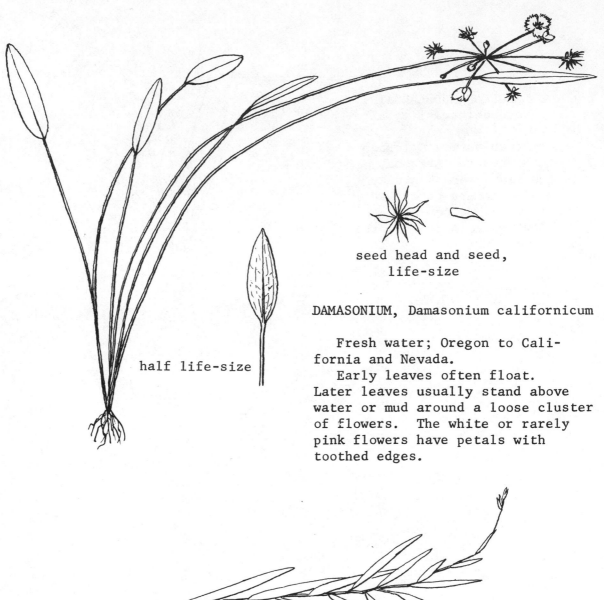

seed head and seed,
life-size

half life-size

DAMASONIUM, Damasonium californicum

Fresh water; Oregon to California and Nevada.
Early leaves often float.
Later leaves usually stand above water or mud around a loose cluster of flowers. The white or rarely pink flowers have petals with toothed edges.

life-size

WATERGRASS, Hydrochloa carolinensis

Fresh water; North Carolina to Louisiana.
Leaves usually float in patches out from shore. Flowers are unlike those of any other plant.
Resembles a few other kinds of small-leaved grasses which are ordinarily out of water, but when temporarily flooded may be under water.

AMPHIANTHUS, Amphianthus pusillus

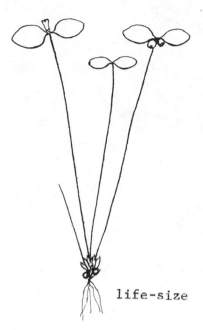

In depressions in granite
which contain water in the spring;
Alabama and Georgia.
    Has a cluster of tiny leaves
and flowers at the base of each
plant, and a pair of larger
floating leaves and a flower or
two at the end of each stem.

life-size

SALVINIA, Salvinia rotundifolia

    A native of tropical America
which has run wild in fresh water
in Georgia and Florida.
    The entire plant floats, with
its roots dangling in the water.
Leaves are concave on the top,
and have coarse hairs standing up
in concentric rows.

half
life-size

two times
life-size

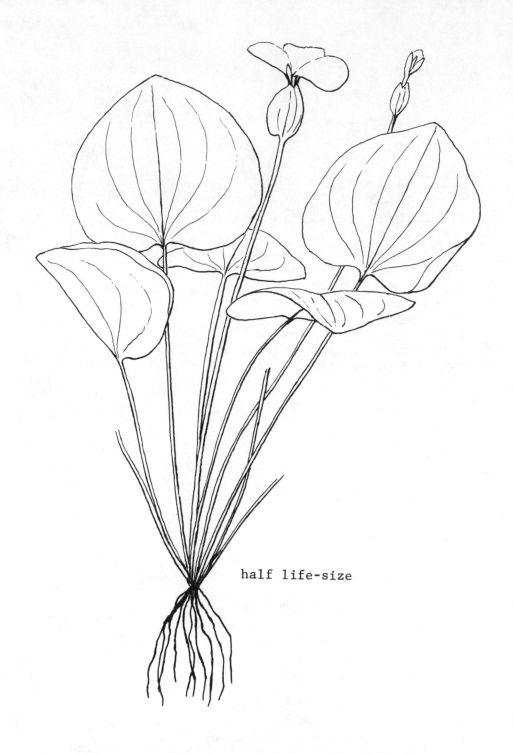

half life-size

OTTELIA, Ottelia alismoides

A native of southeastern Asia and of Australia which
has run wild in fresh water in southwestern Louisiana.
Leaves are under water or floating. Flowers are white
or pinkish.

Group 10. <u>PLANTS WITH LANCE-SHAPED TO ROUND FLOATING LEAVES</u> <u>WHICH ARE DEEPLY NOTCHED AT THE BASE; A FEW KINDS ALSO GROWING</u> <u>PARTLY OUT OF WATER</u> grow in fresh inland water and in fresh to slightly brackish coastal water. The leaves of some kinds are on flexible, upright to horizontal stems; others have leaves coming up from rootstocks. Most kinds have showy flowers: white, yellow, or bluish.

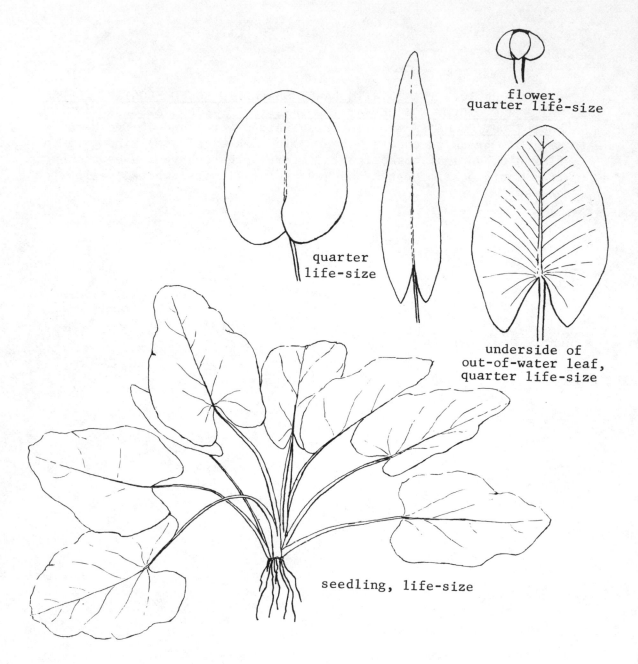

quarter
life-size

flower,
quarter life-size

underside of
out-of-water leaf,
quarter life-size

seedling, life-size

SPATTERDOCK, Nuphar luteum
(all Nuphar in Fernald's and Mason's manuals; all Nymphaea in Small's manual)

Fresh water, inland and coastal; Alaska to Newfoundland, California, and Florida.
Leaves of mature plants roundish to lance-shaped, long-stalked; floating or standing above water (the latter form common along the coast from New York to Virginia). Flowers greenish outside and yellowish to reddish inside.
Leaves of seedlings flimsy and clustered under water. Seedlings resemble those of White Waterlily (page 105), with which they often grow; but Spatterdock leaves have blunter tips and a midvein with several veins on each side.

FLOATING CALTHA,
Caltha natans

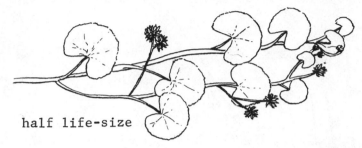

Fresh water;
Alaska to North-
west Territories,
Alberta, and
Wisconsin.
Flowers white
or pinkish.

half life-size

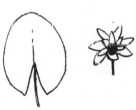

seed pods,
life-size

NORTHERN WATERLILY,
Nymphaea tetragona

Fresh water;
Alaska to Quebec,
Washington, Minne-
sota, and Maine.
Leaves of mature
plants longer than
wide. Flowers
white.

quarter life-size

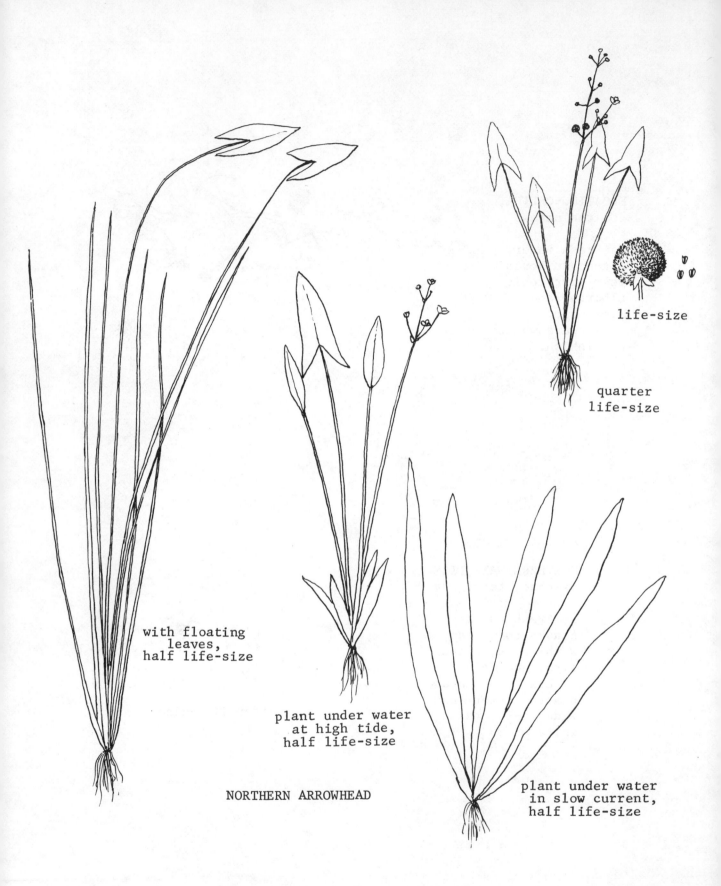

with floating
leaves,
half life-size

plant under water
at high tide,
half life-size

NORTHERN ARROWHEAD

life-size

quarter
life-size

plant under water
in slow current,
half life-size

104

NORTHERN ARROWHEAD, Sagittaria cuneata

Fresh water; Alaska to Quebec, California, Texas, and Connecticut.
Sometimes has long-stalked, arrowhead-shaped floating leaves; but mature plants usually have their leaves and loose clusters of 3-petaled white flowers partly or entirely out of water. The lower flowers produce balls of tight-packed, flattish seeds.
Young plants are clumps of short and stiff to long and ribbonlike underwater leaves which cannot surely be told from some of the Arrowheads described and pictured on pages 18-20. When the leaves are ribbonlike, they can be told from the similar plants of Wildcelery, Burreeds, or Wildrice by holding a piece of leaf to the light and comparing it with the piece-of-leaf picture of Water Arrowhead on page 21 and the pictures on pages 6, 7, and 10.

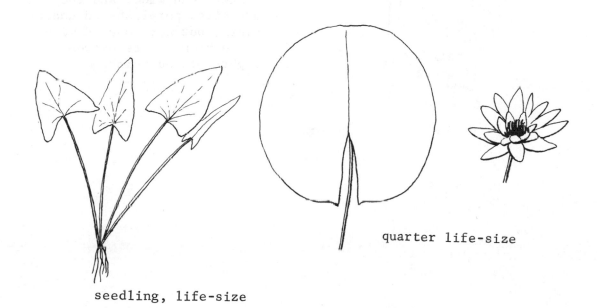

quarter life-size

seedling, life-size

WHITE WATERLILY, Nymphaea odorata
(Nymphaea tuberosa; Castalia lekophylla, minor, and odorata)

Fresh water; Manitoba to Newfoundland, Texas, and Florida.
Leaves of mature plants firm and usually floating. Leaves of seedlings flimsy and clustered under water. Flowers white or rarely pink.
Seedlings of all the Waterlilies resemble each other; but usually only one kind grows in a locality. White Waterlily seedlings resemble Spatterdock seedlings (page 102), with which they often grow; but Waterlily leaves have sharper tips, and most of the veins radiate from near the base.

105

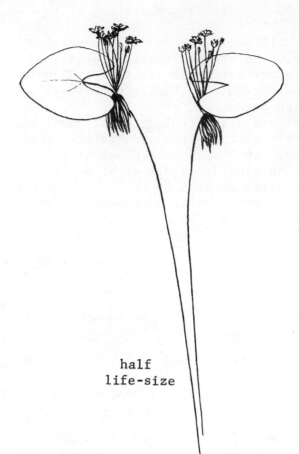

LITTLE FLOATINGHEART,
Nymphoides cordatum
(Nymphoides lacunosum)

Fresh water; Ortario to
Newfoundland, Louisiana, and
Florida.
A cluster of white flowers
reaches just out of water;
and a cluster of short, thick
roots dangles from the stalk
just under a leaf.
Resembles Big Floating-
heart (page 109); but the
smaller leaves are a little
longer than wide; and they
are often purplish-red underneath, but not covered with
close-packed dots between
light-colored veins.

half
life-size

EUROPEAN FROGBIT, Hydrocharis morsus-ranae

Not pictured.
Has escaped from cultivation at Ottawa, Ontario; and since
1932 has spread several miles down the Ottawa River and been
found near Montreal, Quebec.
The leaves resemble those of the floating form of American
Frogbit (page 108); but they have almost no central sponginess.
Three-petaled white flowers stand singly a little above the
leaves. They are about 3/4 inch across and are half to two-
thirds the width of a leaf.

106

ROUNDLEAF MUDPLANTAIN,
Heteranthera reniformis

Fresh water, inland
and coastal; Kansas to
Connecticut, Texas,
and Florida.
Leaves under water,
floating, or out of
water. Flowers white
or bluish.

underside

half life-size

YELLOW FLOATINGHEART,
Nymphoides peltatum

Fresh water, in-
land and rarely
coastal; a native of
Europe which has run
wild in a few local-
ities in Washington,
New York, New Jersey,
Missouri, Oklahoma,
and Arkansas.

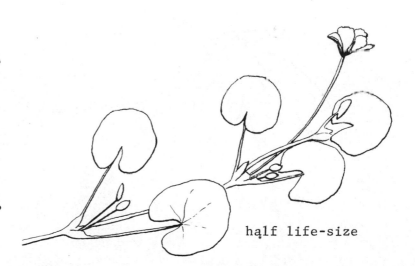

half life-size

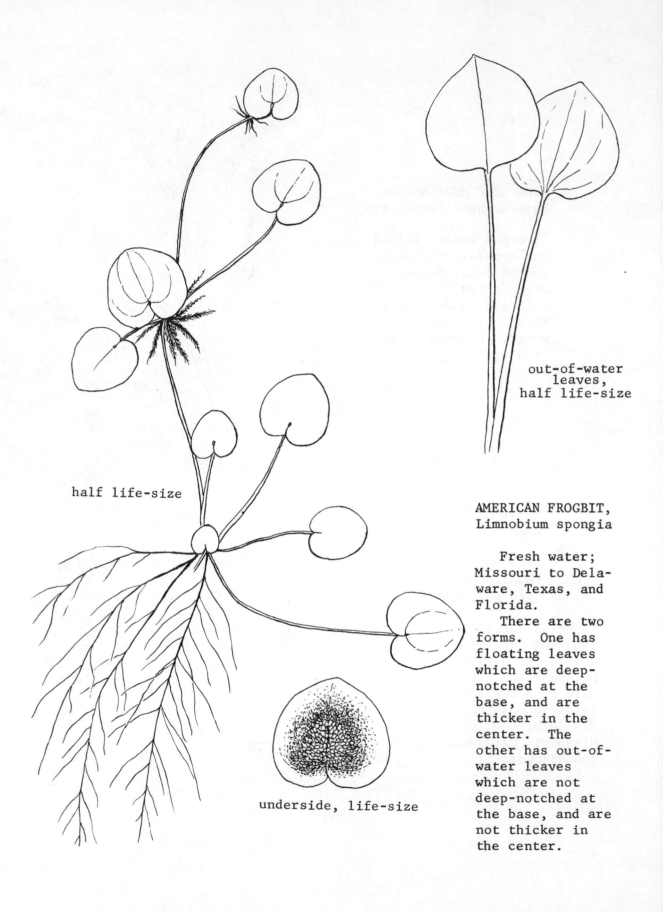

out-of-water
leaves,
half life-size

half life-size

underside, life-size

AMERICAN FROGBIT,
Limnobium spongia

Fresh water;
Missouri to Dela-
ware, Texas, and
Florida.
    There are two
forms. One has
floating leaves
which are deep-
notched at the
base, and are
thicker in the
center. The
other has out-of-
water leaves
which are not
deep-notched at
the base, and are
not thicker in
the center.

108

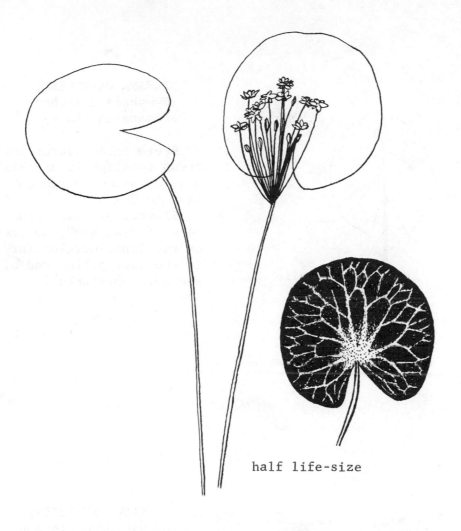

half life-size

BIG FLOATINGHEART, Nymphoides aquaticum

Fresh water; New Jersey to Texas.
A cluster of white flowers reaches just out
of water; and rarely a cluster of short, thick
roots dangles from the stalk just under a leaf.
Resembles Little Floatingheart (page 106);
but the bigger leaves are nearly round, and they
are usually purplish-red with close-packed dots
underneath, except along the light-colored veins.

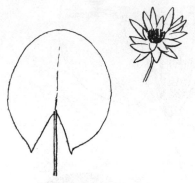

BANANA WATERLILY,
Nymphaea mexicana
(Castalia flava)

Fresh inland water and fresh to slightly brackish coastal water; North Carolina to Texas.

Flowers yellow. Clusters of "bananas", an inch or two long, develop late in the year at the end of slender rootstocks.

quarter life-size

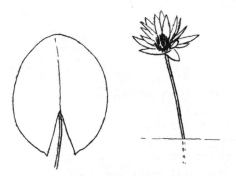

BLUE WATERLILY,
Nymphaea elegans
(Castalia elegans)

Fresh water; southern Texas (mainly), Louisiana, and Florida.

Bluish or pale-violet flowers stand several inches above the water.

quarter life-size

Group 11. <u>PLANTS WITH COARSE-TOOTHED, LOBED, OR DIVIDED</u>
<u>FLOATING LEAVES; SOME KINDS ALSO GROWING PARTLY OUT OF WATER</u> grow in
fresh inland water and rarely in fresh coastal water. The leaves of
Marsileas come up from rootstocks. Those of the other plants are on
flexible, upright to horizontal stems.

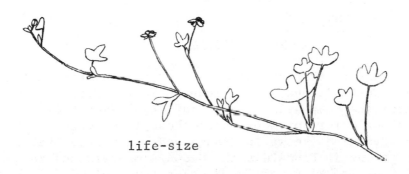

life-size

ARCTIC BUTTERCUP, Ranunculus hyperboreus

Fresh inland water and fresh to brackish
coastal water; Alaska to Greenland, Montana,
and Newfoundland.
Leaves floating or growing partly to
entirely out of water. Flowers yellow.

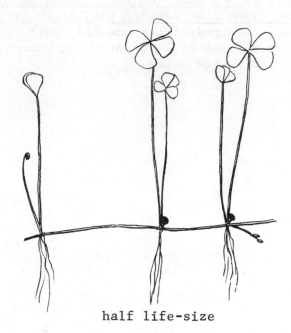

half life-size

MARSILEAS, Marsilea

Fresh water; British Columbia to Massachusetts, California, and Louisiana (but commonest in the West).

Leaves are composed of four leaflets. They float, stand above water, or grow where these is no water.

The five kinds known in Canada and the United States are described in Fernald's and Mason's manuals and in John Kunkel Small's "Flora of the Southeastern United States" (1913) as Marsilea macropoda, mucronata, quadrifolia, tenuifolia, and uncinata. Mucronata, by far the commonest, grows in southwestern Canada and the western half of the United States. Quadrifolia, a native of Europe, has run wild in a few places in the northeastern quarter of the United States. The others have been found only in Texas and neighboring states.

Tenuifolia has very narrow leaflets. The others have wide leaflets, similar to those pictured of mucronata. They can be told apart when they are bearing little bean-shaped sporocarps close to the base of leaf stalks.

112

IVYLEAF BUTTERCUP,
Ranunculus hederaceus

This native of Europe has
been found in fresh water in
a few localities from Newfoundland to South Carolina.
Leaves floating or grow-
ing partly or entirely out
of water. Flowers white.

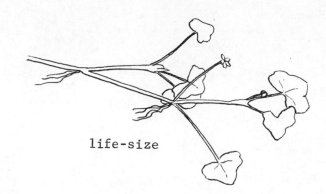

life-size

FLOATING BUTTERCUP,
Ranunculus natans

Fresh water; Alberta to
Colorado.
Leaves floating or grow-
ing partly or entirely out
of water. Flowers yellow.

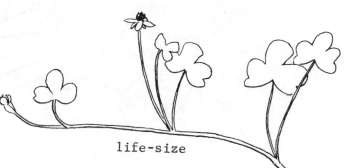

life-size

LOBB BUTTERCUP,
Ranunculus lobbii

In pools which contain
water in the spring;
British Columbia to Cali-
fornia.
Most of the leaves
float. Sometimes there
are fine-forked under-
water leaves. Flowers
white. Seed balls with
no more than 6 seeds
apiece.
Resembles White Water
Buttercup (page 53); but
has mainly floating
leaves and fewer seeds
in a ball.

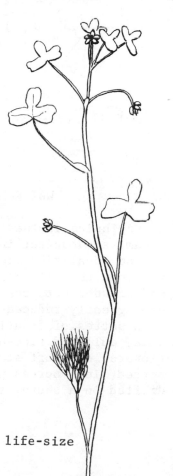

life-size

113

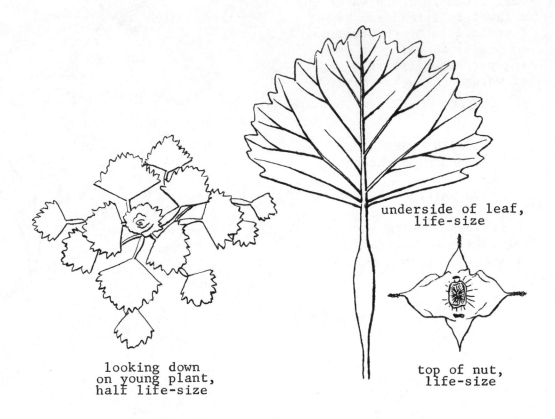

underside of leaf,
life-size

looking down
on young plant,
half life-size

top of nut,
life-size

WATERCHESTNUT, Trapa natans

    Beginning in the 1930's, this native of Eurasia
became so abundant in fresh water in a few coastal and
inland localities from New York to Massachusetts and
Virginia that it spoiled boating, fishing, and swimming,
and crowded out duck-food plants. In some places it has
been greatly reduced by cutting and chemicals.
    Rosettes of floating leaves are shiny on the upper
side, dull and fine-hairy underneath. Small white
flowers, on short stalks among the leaves, produce sharp-
horned, inch-across nuts which, fallen to the bottom or
drifted on a shore, stab bare feet.

Group 12. <u>LITTLE, FREE-FLOATING PLANTS</u> grow in sheltered fresh water, often in the shade of trees, shrubs, and marsh plants. Reproduction is mainly by offshoots from growing plants.

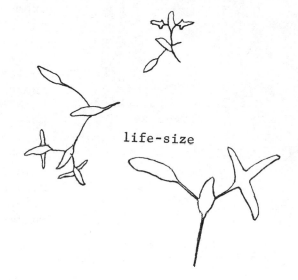

life-size

STAR DUCKWEED, Lemna trisulca

Fresh water; Alaska to Quebec, California, and Georgia (but rare in the southeastern states).
Half-floats under the surface of water which is sheltered from wind and which contains much nitrogenous matter; often under a blanket of Duckweeds and Watermeals. Dull-green. New plants grow from old ones; and several individuals are often attached to each other.

LITTLE DUCKWEEDS, Lemna
(except Lemna trisulca, above)

Fresh water; Alaska to Quebec, California, and Florida.
A green blanket on water which is sheltered from wind and which contains much nitrogenous matter; often mixed with Big Duckweeds and Watermeals. New plants grow from old ones; and a few individuals are often attached to each other. One root dangles in the water from each plant.
The five kinds known in Canada and the United States cannot surely be told apart without a hand lens or microscope, and then only when they have seeds. They are Lemna gibba, minima, minor, perpusilla (trinervis), and valdiviana (cyclostasa).

life-size

115

BIG DUCKWEEDS, Spirodela

Fresh water; British Columbia to Nova Scotia, California, and Florida.

A green blanket on water which is sheltered from wind and which contains much nitrogenous matter; often mixed with Little Duckweeds and Watermeals. Green above, often reddish underneath. New plants grow from old ones; and a few individuals are often attached to each other. A cluster of roots dangles in the water from each plant.

Two kinds are known in Canada and the United States. Spirodela polyrhiza has the range given above, and is the commonest. Each plant usually has 6 or more roots. Spirodela oligorhiza (not pictured) is a native of southeastern Asia and Australia which, since the 1930's, has been found wild in California; and from Missouri to Maryland, Louisiana, and Florida. It is about the same size and shape as the Little Duckweeds (page 115), and each plant usually has only 2 or 3 roots.

Spirodela polyrhiza,
life-size

WATERMEALS, Wolffia

Fresh water; Oregon, California, and Utah; and Nebraska to Quebec, Texas, and Florida.

A green blanket on water which is sheltered from wind and which contains much nitrogenous matter; often mixed with Duckweeds. Individual plants are the size of a small pinhead. New plants grow from old ones; and two individuals are often attached to each other.

The five kinds known in Canada and the United States cannot surely be told apart without a hand lens or microscope. They are Wolffia arrhiza, columbiana (Bruneria columbiana), cylindracea, papulifera, and punctata (Bruneria punctata). The pictures show differences which can sometimes be seen with the naked eye: the round type is light-green all over; the oval type floats on the water like a boat, and is darker green on the top than it is underneath.

two times
life-size

116

RICCIA, Riccia fluitans

Fresh water, British Columbia to Maine, California, and Florida.
Half-floats under the surface of water which is sheltered from wind and which contains much nitrogenous matter; often under a blanket of Duckweeds.

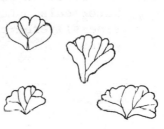

life-size

RICCIOCARPUS, Ricciocarpus natans

Fresh water, British Columbia to Maine, California, and Florida.
On water which is sheltered from wind and which contains much nitrogenous matter; often mixed with Duckweeds. Underside covered with dark-reddish, dangling, rootlike scales.

life-size

WATER-VELVETS, Azolla

Fresh water; British Columbia to Idaho, California, and New Mexico; and Minnesota to New Hampshire, Texas, and Florida.
A dull-green to reddish blanket on water which is sheltered from wind and which contains much nitrogenous matter.
The three kinds known in Canada and the United States cannot surely be told apart without a hand lens or microscope. They are Azolla caroliniana, filiculoides, and mexicana.

two times
life-size

EASTERN WOLFFIELLA,
Wolffiella floridana

    Fresh water; Illinois to
Massachusetts, Texas, and
Florida (but commonest in
the southeastern states).
    Half-floats under the
surface of water which is
sheltered from wind and
which contains much nitrogenous matter; often under
a blanket of Duckweeds and
Watermeals. Looks like
fine-slivered pieces of
grass.

life-size

TONGUE WOLFFIELLA,
Wolffiella lingulata

    Fresh water; California
and Louisiana.
    Half-floats under the
surface of the water.

life-size

118

INDEX

122

A CATALOGUE OF SELECTED DOVER BOOKS
IN ALL FIELDS OF INTEREST

A CATALOGUE OF SELECTED DOVER BOOKS
IN ALL FIELDS OF INTEREST

THE NOTEBOOKS OF LEONARDO DA VINCI, edited by J.P. Richter. Extracts from manuscripts reveal great genius; on painting, sculpture, anatomy, sciences, geography, etc. Both Italian and English. 186 ms. pages reproduced, plus 500 additional drawings, including studies for Last Supper, Sforza monument, etc. 860pp. 7⅞ x 10¾.   USO 22572-0, 22573-9 Pa., Two vol. set $15.90

ART NOUVEAU DESIGNS IN COLOR, Alphonse Mucha, Maurice Verneuil, Georges Auriol. Full-color reproduction of Combinaisons ornamentales (c. 1900) by Art Nouveau masters. Floral, animal, geometric, interlacings, swashes — borders, frames, spots — all incredibly beautiful. 60 plates, hundreds of designs. 9⅜ x 8¹/₁₆ .   22885-1 Pa. $4.00

GRAPHIC WORKS OF ODILON REDON. All great fantastic lithographs, etchings, engravings, drawings, 209 in all. Monsters, Huysmans, still life work, etc. Introduction by Alfred Werner. 209pp. 9⅛ x 12¼.   21996-8 Pa. $6.00

EXOTIC FLORAL PATTERNS IN COLOR, E.-A. Seguy. Incredibly beautiful full-color pochoir work by great French designer of 20's. Complete Bouquets et frondaisons, Suggestions pour étoffes. Richness must be seen to be believed. 40 plates containing 120 patterns. 80pp. 9⅜ x 12¼.   23041-4 Pa. $6.00

SELECTED ETCHINGS OF JAMES A. McN. WHISTLER, James A. McN. Whistler. 149 outstanding etchings by the great American artist, including selections from the Thames set and two Venice sets, the complete French set, and many individual prints. Introduction and explanatory note on each print by Maria Naylor. 157pp. 9⅜ x 12¼.   23194-1 Pa. $5.00

VISUAL ILLUSIONS: THEIR CAUSES, CHARACTERISTICS, AND APPLICATIONS, Matthew Luckiesh. Thorough description, discussion; shape and size, color, motion; natural illusion. Uses in art and industry. 100 illustrations. 252pp.
21530-X Pa. $2.50

TEN BOOKS ON ARCHITECTURE, Vitruvius. The most important book ever written on architecture. Early Roman aesthetics, technology, classical orders, site selection, all other aspects. Stands behind everything since. Morgan translation. 331pp.
20645-9 Pa. $3.50

THE CODEX NUTTALL. A PICTURE MANUSCRIPT FROM ANCIENT MEXICO, as first edited by Zelia Nuttall. Only inexpensive edition, in full color, of a pre-Columbian Mexican (Mixtec) book. 88 color plates show kings, gods, heroes, temples, sacrifices. New explanatory, historical introduction by Arthur G. Miller. 96pp. 11⅜ x 8½.   23168-2 Pa. $7.50

AUSTRIAN COOKING AND BAKING, Gretel Beer. Authentic thick soups, wiener schnitzel, veal goulash, more, plus dumplings, puff pastries, nut cakes, sacher tortes, other great Austrian desserts. 224pp. USO 23220-4 Pa. $2.50

CHEESES OF THE WORLD, U.S.D.A. Dictionary of cheeses containing descriptions of over 400 varieties of cheese from common Cheddar to exotic Surati. Up to two pages are given to important cheeses like Camembert, Cottage, Edam, etc. 151pp. 22831-2 Pa. $1.50

TRITTON'S GUIDE TO BETTER WINE AND BEER MAKING FOR BEGINNERS, S.M. Tritton. All you need to know to make family-sized quantities of over 100 types of grape, fruit, herb, vegetable wines; plus beers, mead, cider, more. 11 illustrations. 157pp. USO 22528-3 Pa. $2.25

DECORATIVE LABELS FOR HOME CANNING, PRESERVING, AND OTHER HOUSEHOLD AND GIFT USES, Theodore Menten. 128 gummed, perforated labels, beautifully printed in 2 colors. 12 versions in traditional, Art Nouveau, Art Deco styles. Adhere to metal, glass, wood, most plastics. 24pp. 8¼ x 11. 23219-0 Pa. $2.00

FIVE ACRES AND INDEPENDENCE, Maurice G. Kains. Great back-to-the-land classic explains basics of self-sufficient farming: economics, plants, crops, animals, orchards, soils, land selection, host of other necessary things. Do not confuse with skimpy faddist literature; Kains was one of America's greatest agriculturalists. 95 illustrations. 397pp. 20974-1 Pa. $3.00

GROWING VEGETABLES IN THE HOME GARDEN, U.S. Dept. of Agriculture. Basic information on site, soil conditions, selection of vegetables, planting, cultivation, gathering. Up-to-date, concise, authoritative. Covers 60 vegetables. 30 illustrations. 123pp. 23167-4 Pa. $1.35

FRUITS FOR THE HOME GARDEN, Dr. U.P. Hedrick. A chapter covering each type of garden fruit, advice on plant care, soils, grafting, pruning, sprays, transplanting, and much more! Very full. 53 illustrations. 175pp. 22944-0 Pa. $2.50

GARDENING ON SANDY SOIL IN NORTH TEMPERATE AREAS, Christine Kelway. Is your soil too light, too sandy? Improve your soil, select plants that survive under such conditions. Both vegetables and flowers. 42 photos. 148pp. USO 23199-2 Pa. $2.50

THE FRAGRANT GARDEN: A BOOK ABOUT SWEET SCENTED FLOWERS AND LEAVES, Louise Beebe Wilder. Fullest, best book on growing plants for their fragrances. Descriptions of hundreds of plants, both well-known and overlooked. 407pp. 23071-6 Pa. $4.00

EASY GARDENING WITH DROUGHT-RESISTANT PLANTS, Arno and Irene Nehrling. Authoritative guide to gardening with plants that require a minimum of water: seashore, desert, and rock gardens; house plants; annuals and perennials, much more. 190 illustrations. 320pp. 23230-1 Pa. $3.50

JEWISH GREETING CARDS, Ed Sibbett, Jr. 16 cards to cut and color. Three say "Happy Chanukah," one "Happy New Year," others have no message, show stars of David, Torahs, wine cups, other traditional themes. 16 envelopes. 8¼ x 11.
23225-5 Pa. $2.00

AUBREY BEARDSLEY GREETING CARD BOOK, Aubrey Beardsley. Edited by Theodore Menten. 16 elegant yet inexpensive greeting cards let you combine your own sentiments with subtle Art Nouveau lines. 16 different Aubrey Beardsley designs that you can color or not, as you wish. 16 envelopes. 64pp. 8¼ x 11.
23173-9 Pa. $2.00

RECREATIONS IN THE THEORY OF NUMBERS, Albert Beiler. Number theory, an inexhaustible source of puzzles, recreations, for beginners and advanced. Divisors, perfect numbers. scales of notation, etc. 349pp.
21096-0 Pa. $4.00

AMUSEMENTS IN MATHEMATICS, Henry E. Dudeney. One of largest puzzle collections, based on algebra, arithmetic, permutations, probability, plane figure dissection, properties of numbers, by one of world's foremost puzzlists. Solutions. 450 illustrations. 258pp.
20473-1 Pa. $3.00

MATHEMATICS, MAGIC AND MYSTERY, Martin Gardner. Puzzle editor for Scientific American explains math behind: card tricks, stage mind reading, coin and match tricks, counting out games, geometric dissections. Probability, sets, theory of numbers, clearly explained. Plus more than 400 tricks, guaranteed to work. 135 illustrations. 176pp.
20335-2 Pa. $2.00

BEST MATHEMATICAL PUZZLES OF SAM LOYD, edited by Martin Gardner. Bizarre, original, whimsical puzzles by America's greatest puzzler. From fabulously rare Cyclopedia, including famous 14-15 puzzles, the Horse of a Different Color, 115 more. Elementary math. 150 illustrations. 167pp.
20498-7 Pa. $2.50

MATHEMATICAL PUZZLES FOR BEGINNERS AND ENTHUSIASTS, Geoffrey Mott-Smith. 189 puzzles from easy to difficult involving arithmetic, logic, algebra, properties of digits, probability. Explanation of math behind puzzles. 135 illustrations. 248pp.
20198-8 Pa. $2.75

BIG BOOK OF MAZES AND LABYRINTHS, Walter Shepherd. Classical, solid, and ripple mazes; short path and avoidance labyrinths; more — 50 mazes and labyrinths in all. 12 other figures. Full solutions. 112pp. 8⅛ x 11.
22951-3 Pa. $2.00

COIN GAMES AND PUZZLES, Maxey Brooke. 60 puzzles, games and stunts — from Japan, Korea, Africa and the ancient world, by Dudeney and the other great puzzlers, as well as Maxey Brooke's own creations. Full solutions. 67 illustrations. 94pp.
22893-2 Pa. $1.50

HAND SHADOWS TO BE THROWN UPON THE WALL, Henry Bursill. Wonderful Victorian novelty tells how to make flying birds, dog, goose, deer, and 14 others. 32pp. 6½ x 9¼.
21779-5 Pa. $1.25

COOKIES FROM MANY LANDS, Josephine Perry. Crullers, oatmeal cookies, chaux au chocolate, English tea cakes, mandel kuchen, Sacher torte, Danish puff pastry, Swedish cookies — a mouth-watering collection of 223 recipes. 157pp.
22832-0 Pa. $2.00

ROSE RECIPES, Eleanour S. Rohde. How to make sauces, jellies, tarts, salads, pot-pourris, sweet bags, pomanders, perfumes from garden roses; all exact recipes. Century old favorites. 95pp.
22957-2 Pa. $1.25

"OSCAR" OF THE WALDORF'S COOKBOOK, Oscar Tschirky. Famous American chef reveals 3455 recipes that made Waldorf great; cream of French, German, American cooking, in all categories. Full instructions, easy home use. 1896 edition. 907pp. 6⅝ x 9⅜ .
20790-0 Clothbd. $15.00

JAMS AND JELLIES, May Byron. Over 500 old-time recipes for delicious jams, jellies, marmalades, preserves, and many other items. Probably the largest jam and jelly book in print. Originally titled May Byron's Jam Book. 276pp.
USO 23130-5 Pa. $3.00

MUSHROOM RECIPES, André L. Simon. 110 recipes for everyday and special cooking. Champignons à la grecque, sole bonne femme, chicken liver croustades, more; 9 basic sauces, 13 ways of cooking mushrooms. 54pp.
USO 20913-X Pa. $1.25

FAVORITE SWEDISH RECIPES, edited by Sam Widenfelt. Prepared in Sweden, offers wonderful, clearly explained Swedish dishes: appetizers, meats, pastry and cookies, other categories. Suitable for American kitchen. 90 photos. 157pp.
23156-9 Pa. $2.00

THE BUCKEYE COOKBOOK, Buckeye Publishing Company. Over 1,000 easy-to-follow, traditional recipes from the American Midwest: bread (100 recipes alone), meat, game, jam, candy, cake, ice cream, and many other categories of cooking. 64 illustrations. From 1883 enlarged edition. 416pp.
23218-2 Pa. $4.00

TWENTY-TWO AUTHENTIC BANQUETS FROM INDIA, Robert H. Christie. Complete, easy-to-do recipes for almost 200 authentic Indian dishes assembled in 22 banquets. Arranged by region. Selected from Banquets of the Nations. 192pp.
23200-X Pa. $2.50

SLEEPING BEAUTY, illustrated by Arthur Rackham. Perhaps the fullest, most delightful version ever, told by C.S. Evans. Rackham's best work. 49 illustrations. 110pp. 7⅞ x 10¾. 22756-1 Pa. **$2.00**

THE WONDERFUL WIZARD OF OZ, L. Frank Baum. Facsimile in full color of America's finest children's classic. Introduction by Martin Gardner. 143 illustrations by W.W. Denslow. 267pp. 20691-2 Pa. **$3.00**

GOOPS AND HOW TO BE THEM, Gelett Burgess. Classic tongue-in-cheek masquerading as etiquette book. 87 verses, 170 cartoons as Goops demonstrate virtues of table manners, neatness, courtesy, more. 88pp. 6½ x 9¼.
22233-0 Pa. **$2.00**

THE BROWNIES, THEIR BOOK, Palmer Cox. Small as mice, cunning as foxes, exuberant, mischievous, Brownies go to zoo, toy shop, seashore, circus, more. 24 verse adventures. 266 illustrations. 144pp. 6⅝ x 9¼. 21265-3 Pa. **$2.50**

BILLY WHISKERS: THE AUTOBIOGRAPHY OF A GOAT, Frances Trego Montgomery. Escapades of that rambunctious goat. Favorite from turn of the century America. 24 illustrations. 259pp. 22345-0 Pa. $2.75

THE ROCKET BOOK, Peter Newell. Fritz, janitor's kid, sets off rocket in basement of apartment house; an ingenious hole punched through every page traces course of rocket. 22 duotone drawings, verses. 48pp. 6⅞ x 8⅜. 22044-3 Pa. $1.50

PECK'S BAD BOY AND HIS PA, George W. Peck. Complete double-volume of great American childhood classic. Hennery's ingenious pranks against outraged pomposity of pa and the grocery man. 97 illustrations. Introduction by E.F. Bleiler. 347pp. 20497-9 Pa. $2.50

THE TALE OF PETER RABBIT, Beatrix Potter. The inimitable Peter's terrifying adventure in Mr. McGregor's garden, with all 27 wonderful, full-color Potter illustrations. 55pp. 4¼ x 5½. USO 22827-4 Pa. $1.00

THE TALE OF MRS. TIGGY-WINKLE, Beatrix Potter. Your child will love this story about a very special hedgehog and all 27 wonderful, full-color Potter illustrations. 57pp. 4¼ x 5½. USO 20546-0 Pa. $1.00

THE TALE OF BENJAMIN BUNNY, Beatrix Potter. Peter Rabbit's cousin coaxes him back into Mr. McGregor's garden for a whole new set of adventures. A favorite with children. All 27 full-color illustrations. 59pp. 4¼ x 5½.
USO 21102-9 Pa. $1.00

THE MERRY ADVENTURES OF ROBIN HOOD, Howard Pyle. Facsimile of original (1883) edition, finest modern version of English outlaw's adventures. 23 illustrations by Pyle. 296pp. 6½ x 9¼. 22043-5 Pa. **$4.00**

TWO LITTLE SAVAGES, Ernest Thompson Seton. Adventures of two boys who lived as Indians; explaining Indian ways, woodlore, pioneer methods. 293 illustrations. 286pp. 20985-7 Pa. $3.00

MANUAL OF THE TREES OF NORTH AMERICA, Charles S. Sargent. The basic survey of every native tree and tree-like shrub, 717 species in all. Extremely full descriptions, information on habitat, growth, locales, economics, etc. Necessary to every serious tree lover. Over 100 finding keys. 783 illustrations. Total of 986pp.
20277-1, 20278-X Pa., Two vol. set $9.00

BIRDS OF THE NEW YORK AREA, John Bull. Indispensable guide to more than 400 species within a hundred-mile radius of Manhattan. Information on range, status, breeding, migration, distribution trends, etc. Foreword by Roger Tory Peterson. 17 drawings; maps. 540pp.
23222-0 Pa. $6.00

THE SEA-BEACH AT EBB-TIDE, Augusta Foote Arnold. Identify hundreds of marine plants and animals: algae, seaweeds, squids, crabs, corals, etc. Descriptions cover food, life cycle, size, shape, habitat. Over 600 drawings. 490pp.
21949-6 Pa. $5.00

THE MOTH BOOK, William J. Holland. Identify more than 2,000 moths of North America. General information, precise species descriptions. 623 illustrations plus 48 color plates show almost all species, full size. 1968 edition. Still the basic book. Total of 551pp. 6½ x 9¼.
21948-8 Pa. $6.00

AN INTRODUCTION TO THE REPTILES AND AMPHIBIANS OF THE UNITED STATES, Percy A. Morris. All lizards, crocodiles, turtles, snakes, toads, frogs; life history, identification, habits, suitability as pets, etc. Non-technical, but sound and broad. 130 photos. 253pp.
22982-3 Pa. $3.00

OLD NEW YORK IN EARLY PHOTOGRAPHS, edited by Mary Black. Your only chance to see New York City as it was 1853-1906, through 196 wonderful photographs from N.Y. Historical Society. Great Blizzard, Lincoln's funeral procession, great buildings. 228pp. 9 x 12.
22907-6 Pa. $6.00

THE AMERICAN REVOLUTION, A PICTURE SOURCEBOOK, John Grafton. Wonderful Bicentennial picture source, with 411 illustrations (contemporary and 19th century) showing battles, personalities, maps, events, flags, posters, soldier's life, ships, etc. all captioned and explained. A wonderful browsing book, supplement to other historical reading. 160pp. 9 x 12.
23226-3 Pa. $4.00

PERSONAL NARRATIVE OF A PILGRIMAGE TO AL-MADINAH AND MECCAH, Richard Burton. Great travel classic by remarkably colorful personality. Burton, disguised as a Moroccan, visited sacred shrines of Islam, narrowly escaping death. Wonderful observations of Islamic life, customs, personalities. 47 illustrations. Total of 959pp.
21217-3, 21218-1 Pa., Two vol. set $10.00

INCIDENTS OF TRAVEL IN CENTRAL AMERICA, CHIAPAS, AND YUCATAN, John L. Stephens. Almost single-handed discovery of Maya culture; exploration of ruined cities, monuments, temples; customs of Indians. 115 drawings. 892pp.
22404-X, 22405-8 Pa., Two vol. set $8.00

DECORATIVE ALPHABETS AND INITIALS, edited by Alexander Nesbitt. 91 complete alphabets (medieval to modern), 3924 decorative initials, including Victorian novelty and Art Nouveau. 192pp. 7¾ x 10¾. 20544-4 Pa. $4.00

CALLIGRAPHY, Arthur Baker. Over 100 original alphabets from the hand of our greatest living calligrapher: simple, bold, fine-line, richly ornamented, etc. —all strikingly original and different, a fusion of many influences and styles. 155pp. 11⅜ x 8¼. 22895-9 Pa. $4.50

MONOGRAMS AND ALPHABETIC DEVICES, edited by Hayward and Blanche Cirker. Over 2500 combinations, names, crests in very varied styles: script engraving, ornate Victorian, simple Roman, and many others. 226pp. 8⅛ x 11.
22330-2 Pa. $5.00

THE BOOK OF SIGNS, Rudolf Koch. Famed German type designer renders 493 symbols: religious, alchemical, imperial, runes, property marks, etc. Timeless. 104pp. 6⅛ x 9¼. 20162-7 Pa. $1.75

200 DECORATIVE TITLE PAGES, edited by Alexander Nesbitt. 1478 to late 1920's. Baskerville, Dürer, Beardsley, W. Morris, Pyle, many others in most varied techniques. For posters, programs, other uses. 222pp. 8⅜ x 11¼. 21264-5 Pa. **$5.00**

DICTIONARY OF AMERICAN PORTRAITS, edited by Hayward and Blanche Cirker. 4000 important Americans, earliest times to 1905, mostly in clear line. Politicians, writers, soldiers, scientists, inventors, industrialists, Indians, Blacks, women, outlaws, etc. Identificatory information. 756pp. 9¼ x 12¾. 21823-6 Clothbd. $30.00

ART FORMS IN NATURE, Ernst Haeckel. Multitude of strangely beautiful natural forms: Radiolaria, Foraminifera, jellyfishes, fungi, turtles, bats, etc. All 100 plates of the 19th century evolutionist's Kunstformen der Natur (1904). 100pp. 9⅜ x 12¼. 22987-4 Pa. $4.00

DECOUPAGE: THE BIG PICTURE SOURCEBOOK, Eleanor Rawlings. Make hundreds of beautiful objects, over 550 florals, animals, letters, shells, period costumes, frames, etc. selected by foremost practitioner. Printed on one side of page. 8 color plates. Instructions. 176pp. 9³⁄₁₆ x 12¼. 23182-8 Pa. $5.00

AMERICAN FOLK DECORATION, Jean Lipman, Eve Meulendyke. Thorough coverage of all aspects of wood, tin, leather, paper, cloth decoration — scapes, humans, trees, flowers, geometrics — and how to make them. Full instructions. 233 illustrations, 5 in color. 163pp. 8⅜ x 11¼. 22217-9 Pa. $3.95

WHITTLING AND WOODCARVING, E.J. Tangerman. Best book on market; clear, full. If you can cut a potato, you can carve toys, puzzles, chains, caricatures, masks, patterns, frames, decorate surfaces, etc. Also covers serious wood sculpture. Over 200 photos. 293pp. 20965-2 Pa. $3.00

HOW TO SOLVE CHESS PROBLEMS, Kenneth S. Howard. Practical suggestions on problem solving for very beginners. 58 two-move problems, 46 3-movers, 8 4-movers for practice, plus hints. 171pp. 20748-X Pa. $2.00

A GUIDE TO FAIRY CHESS, Anthony Dickins. 3-D chess, 4-D chess, chess on a cylindrical board, reflecting pieces that bounce off edges, cooperative chess, retrograde chess, maximummers, much more. Most based on work of great Dawson. Full handbook, 100 problems. 66pp. 7⅞ x 10¾. 22687-5 Pa. $2.00

WIN AT BACKGAMMON, Millard Hopper. Best opening moves, running game, blocking game, back game, tables of odds, etc. Hopper makes the game clear enough for anyone to play, and win. 43 diagrams. 111pp. 22894-0 Pa. $1.50

BIDDING A BRIDGE HAND, Terence Reese. Master player "thinks out loud" the binding of 75 hands that defy point count systems. Organized by bidding problem—no-fit situations, overbidding, underbidding, cueing your defense, etc. 254pp. EBE 22830-4 Pa. $3.00

THE PRECISION BIDDING SYSTEM IN BRIDGE, C.C. Wei, edited by Alan Truscott. Inventor of precision bidding presents average hands and hands from actual play, including games from 1969 Bermuda Bowl where system emerged. 114 exercises. 116pp. 21171-1 Pa. $1.75

LEARN MAGIC, Henry Hay. 20 simple, easy-to-follow lessons on magic for the new magician: illusions, card tricks, silks, sleights of hand, coin manipulations, escapes, and more —all with a minimum amount of equipment. Final chapter explains the great stage illusions. 92 illustrations. 285pp. 21238-6 Pa. $2.95

THE NEW MAGICIAN'S MANUAL, Walter B. Gibson. Step-by-step instructions and clear illustrations guide the novice in mastering 36 tricks; much equipment supplied on 16 pages of cut-out materials. 36 additional tricks. 64 illustrations. 159pp. 6⅝ x 10. 23113-5 Pa. $3.00

PROFESSIONAL MAGIC FOR AMATEURS, Walter B. Gibson. 50 easy, effective tricks used by professionals —cards, string, tumblers, handkerchiefs, mental magic, etc. 63 illustrations. 223pp. 23012-0 Pa. $2.50

CARD MANIPULATIONS, Jean Hugard. Very rich collection of manipulations; has taught thousands of fine magicians tricks that are really workable, eye-catching. Easily followed, serious work. Over 200 illustrations. 163pp. 20539-8 Pa. $2.00

ABBOTT'S ENCYCLOPEDIA OF ROPE TRICKS FOR MAGICIANS, Stewart James. Complete reference book for amateur and professional magicians containing more than 150 tricks involving knots, penetrations, cut and restored rope, etc. 510 illustrations. Reprint of 3rd edition. 400pp. 23206-9 Pa. $3.50

THE SECRETS OF HOUDINI, J.C. Cannell. Classic study of Houdini's incredible magic, exposing closely-kept professional secrets and revealing, in general terms, the whole art of stage magic. 67 illustrations. 279pp. 22913-0 Pa. $2.50